30-Day Bootcamp:

Your Ultimate Life Makeover

Cheri Baumann

21265 Stevens Creek Blvd., Suite 205
Cupertino, CA 95014

30-Day Bootcamp: Your Ultimate Life Makeover

First Printing, October 2006

Tradebook ISBN 1600050174

eBook ISBN 1600050182

Place of Publication: Silicon Valley, California, USA

Library of Congress Control Number: 2006933699

Trademarks

Warning and Disclaimer

A Message From Happy About®

Thank you for your purchase of this Happy About book. It is available online at **http://happyabout.info/30daybootcamp/life-makeover.php** or at other online and physical bookstores.

Please contact us for quantity discounts at **sales@happyabout.info**

If you want to be informed by e-mail of upcoming Happy About® books, please e-mail **bookupdate@happyabout.info**

If you want to contribute to upcoming Happy About® books, please go to **http://happyabout.info/contribute/**

Happy About is interested in you if you are an author that would like to submit a non-fiction book proposal or a corporation that would like to have a book written for you. Please contact us by e-mail **editorial@happyabout.info** or phone **(1-408-257-3000)**.

Other Happy About® books available include:

Happy About Global Software Test Automation:
http://happyabout.info/globalswtestautomation.php

Happy About Joint Venturing:
http://happyabout.info/jointventuring.php

Happy About LinkedIn for Recruiting:
http://happyabout.info/linkedin4recruiting.php

Happy About Website Payments with PayPal:
http://happyabout.info/paypal.php

Happy About Outsourcing:
http://happyabout.info/outsourcing.php

Happy About Knowing What to Expect in 2006:
http://happyabout.info/economy.php

Other soon-to-be-released Happy About® books include:

Happy About CEO Excellence:
http://happyabout.info/ceo-excellence.php

Happy About Working After 60:
http://happyabout.info/working-after-60.php

Happy About Open Source:
http://happyabout.info/opensource.php

A Message From My Private Coach

MyPrivateCoach is a Silicon Valley company whose mission is to help the general public reach their personal development goals through coaching programs, which, in the past, were only available to the wealthy, celebrities and top athletes.

MyPrivateCoach is a major actor of the personal development market, offering expert coaching programs in four distinct areas: business & executive, health & fitness, life, and relationships. Such programs may be delivered through different channels: face-to-face, telephone, VOIP, instant messenger, email/online and seminars and retreats.

Through this rich set of programs and high tech delivery channels, MyPrivateCoach brings together a core team of 80 carefully selected expert coaches and customers who want to reach their personal Olympic level.

Visit us at **www.MyPrivateCoach.com**

A Message from 30dayBootCamp

The brainchild of MyPrivateCoach's CEO and Founder, Valerie Orsoni-Vauthey, 30dayBootCamp.com is the ultimate online coaching experience for a very affordable price. Here, top international coaches make their expertise available in the areas of Health & Fitness, Business & Executive, Life and Love coaching. The entire program is delivered over web 2.0 including a full suite of interactive video, blogging and VOIP communication tools.

Find all 30dayBootCamp books online at
www.happyabout.info/30daybootcamp/

Acknowledgments

I would like to thank Mitchell Levy, publisher of Happy About Info Books and Valerie Orsini-Vauthey, CEO of www.MyPrivateCoach.com for their encouragement, faith and direction in this project. I also would like to extend a warm thank-you to all of my clients over the years who have helped me perfect the information and exercises offered in this book.

A big thanks also needs to be extended to the 'behind the scenes' people without whom I could not have brought this book to press. I thank Rachel and Jean Baumann for their outstanding proof-reading skills, Selim Sora for his amazing type-setting skills and Alan Roberts for his exceptional editorial skills.

This book has been the culmination of many years of training in psychology, education and coaching, in addition to many years of my own personal growth work. I would therefore be remiss if I did not thank all of the excellent teachers, workshop leaders, coaches and mentors I have had through the years. I thank Randy and Elisabeth Revell for creating all of the outstanding programs offered through Context Associated, Harv Eker for his amazing programs offered through Peak Potentials, and Bennet Wong and Jock Mckeen for creating the safe sanctuary of personal growth at "The Haven". I also would like to thank all of the people I encountered during the many workshops I've participated in, as well as the 'coachees' I had as a coach in training.

Brent Stewart, you were a shining light of motivation and inspiration as I began my personal growth work with the Pursuit of Excellence in 1993. Harv Eker, thanks to your fear blasting exercise offered in the "The Millionaire Mind" workshop where I shyly wrote down "World Class Coach" as my biggest dream back in 2002 – I can now say that I have not only accomplished that dream by being one of the world's leading international coaches, but have surpassed it by being the creator and chief instructor of MyPrivateCoach's International Coach Training and Mentorship Program.

I would not be at the point I am without the love and support of my family and very close friends. Many thanks to my Mom and Dad for their encouraging words even when they thought I was 'crazy' to leave the secure world of teaching for the not so secure world of coaching and writing. I thank my Uncle Frank, who has always been there when I needed him and certainly has loved me through thick and thin. Thank-you also to my two beautiful sisters, Sue and Sandy – although there were times when we were very young that I wish I had been an only child, I feel very blessed to have two sisters who I can call my very best friends.

A special thanks also to my women's support group, otherwise jokingly known as "The Coven." Goody, Lee, Noni, Cathy, Nancy, Sandra and Annette – over the past 12 years we have learned to support each other unconditionally and I would certainly not be the woman I am today without all of your words of wisdom, support and love. I also thank long time friends (some of whom I have not even seen of late) who have left indelible impressions upon my soul – thank-you Neil and Jeannette Mackay as well as Herman and Ilse Reichert (also known as Mama and Papa Reichert) for being in so many ways a second and third set of parents to me. I also give many thanks to Dr. Karen Buhler, June Harrison, Martha Leigh, George Connell and Lee Crawford for the love and support that I have received from you over the years. And a very special thanks to my childhood friend Phyllis Tarrant (I am sorry but I do not know your married name) for all of the laughter, good times, and terrific friendship.

Last, but certainly not least, none of this could have been possible without the unending love and support from my life partner, Alan Roberts. You have been my greatest cheerleader and believed in my abilities even when I did not. Without your support I would not have stepped outside of the box and looked beyond my comfort zone to a life that fully embraces my greatest gifts. I love you.

To my mom and dad,
Jean and Adam Baumann.

Your Ultimate Life Makeover Starts Here!

The Road Map

Do you want to take control of your life? Do you want to live the life of your dreams? Well congratulations because you are already well on your way to doing just that!

Did you know that 80% of success is just showing up? That's right. 80%!

It is no accident that you are reading this book. Your desire to makeover your life along with this SuperU 30-Day Bootcamp has already moved you 80% closer to your dream. And it keeps getting better. Once you start this program you will begin to experience results right away, and these results will continue to grow even after you have created the life of your dreams.

You can transform your life with this ultimate roadmap for success!

Everything you need to literally makeover your entire life is all laid out, in this foolproof, simple and easy to follow structured program. It is based upon proven coaching methods that have worked for thousands of people. And it can work for you too!

Think about it. If you wanted to get the most out of your *finances*, you would seek the advice of an exceptionally qualified financial strategist with a proven track record of success. If you want to get the most out of your *life*, it makes sense that you would seek the advice of an exceptionally qualified life strategist with a proven track record of success.

I am a Certified Master Life Coach and Trainer with over 25 years combined experience as a life coach and educator and I am the creator of this revolutionary program. I have degrees in both psychology and education, am an Associate Coach with the University of British Columbia, and am the Director of Training and Coach Development for the leading worldwide coaching organization: MyPrivateCoach. I specialize as a Life Strategist and a Personal Development Coach and have helped thousands of people just like you, from all over the world, to develop successful life strategies that support who they are, what they want, and where they want to go.

My purpose in life is to create the space for people to recognize who they really are and then BE that person. The 30-Day Bootcamp: Your Ultimate Life Makeover is designed to teach you how to fully embrace WHO you are, the GIFTS you have to give to the world, and to LIVE the life you were meant to live.

You are not alone anymore, together we will succeed!

This amazing program puts you, the Bootcamper, back into the driver's seat of your life and provides you with the roadmap you need to live the life of your dreams. Its workbook format is broken down into 5 logical sections made up of 6 distinct steps. Each section and step builds upon the next, so that by Day 30 you will have created the life you have always wanted to live.

1. Get Ready

We will begin your journey ensuring you have everything you need to embark on your ultimate life makeover. Here you will commit to the process of creating a successful life strategy, lay the groundwork for all of your success and move outside of your comfort zone by blasting through your limitations.

2. Your Starting Point

Now that you have prepared for your journey, it is essential for you to know where it begins. Here you will clearly define what your life is like now in 8 specific areas – your career, your relationship with friends and family, your relationship with your significant partner, your fun and recreation, your health, your personal growth, your finances and your personal environment.

3. Your Ultimate Destination

A successful journey has a starting point and an end point – it is therefore essential that you know exactly where you are headed in order to get to where you want to go. Here you will envision your ideal life in each of the 8 life areas you defined at your starting point.

4. Your Journey

Now that you have a clearly defined starting and end point of your journey, it is time for you determine how you'll get there and your stops along the way. The framework is all laid out for you, all you need to do is fill in the blanks and create the life of your dreams.

5. Keep on Going!

It is essential that even once your 30-Day journey has ended that you maintain your resolve and keep the life of your dreams a priority. Here you will be encouraged to get the support you need to sustain what you have created, and to keep this phenomenal journey alive! You will also be provided with all the tools you need to ensure that you will indeed be able to keep on going.

This program is meant to be followed at your own pace. **For optimum success, I recommend that you choose the amount of time that you will spend on each 'Day', and then stick to it.** For people who want to get results FAST, that means following it each day, for 30 days. For others, who prefer to devote more time and energy to the process, taking two or three days, or even a full week for each 'Day' of the program is absolutely fine. The time it takes you to complete the program is not important. Doing it consistently is.

You will be guaranteed to succeed with this foolproof program. And with me there to guide and motivate you every step of the way, you have nothing to lose and only a "SuperU" Life to gain. So what are you waiting for?

Let's get started NOW!

Get Ready

Success is the outcome of preparation meeting opportunity. Therefore the first secret to creating your ultimate life is to be properly prepared for it.

On days 1 through 6 you will prepare the groundwork for the magnificent journey upon which you are about to embark. You will strengthen your personal core to ensure that you have the inner resources to attract and create the success you desire. You will gain clarity about who you are and what you want, and move out of your comfort zone by blasting through your limitations.

Get ready to "get ready" to get your life on track and live the life of your dreams!

Who is in the Driver's Seat of Your Life?

WHAT would happen if you lived your life by design rather than by default? What would happen if you took the time to choose what you wanted in life, rather than letting life choose it for you?

I am sure many of you know people who are living their lives on autopilot. They get up in the morning, get ready to go to work, drive to work using the same route, do their daily work tasks, drive home from work using the same route as before, eat dinner, perhaps play with the kids, watch TV and then go to bed. The next morning it starts all over again. Before you know it, weeks have gone by, months, and then years.

Sometimes a life crisis happens, a severe accident, a life-threatening illness, the death of a loved one, or a mid-life crisis, and these people who have been on autopilot for so many years suddenly wake-up and take a good look at the lives they have been living. They may realize that they have been 'human doings' rather than 'human beings,' living their lives for everyone and everything other than themselves.

What is ironic about this situation is that whether we like it or not, we are the authors of our own lives. Everything that we have right now is the RESULT of the choices and decisions we have made along the way, even if our choices were made on autopilot or chosen according to some sort of 'should,' 'could,' or 'ought to'. We can too easily get sucked into external expectations and the idea of our own personal and authentic life slips away.

A life crisis is not necessary for making positive changes in your life. Take a good hard look at your life right now and ask yourself:

> ### *"If I am not the one in the driver's seat, then who or what is?"*

Living your life in the driver's seat means that you know what you want and what is most important to you. You live a balanced and fulfilling life filled with purpose and meaning. You have taken the time to create an authentic, vibrant and happy life, because if you don't take the time to choose what you want, life will choose it for you.

The way to get back into the driver's seat of your life is to create a life strategy. If you want to get the most out of your money you must create a financial strategy. The same is true for your life.

The first two important steps in creating a successful life strategy are committing to it and developing a strong personal core.

1. Commit to it.

As mentioned before, you are the author of your own life – the artist of your own creation. It has taken a considerable amount of time to create the life you have now.

It makes sense then to think that change cannot happen overnight. You are going to have to be willing to commit to the process of designing the kind of life you want. This is going to require some time to reflect on what your life is like now, how you want it to be, and then planning and taking specific action steps to implement the changes you want.

2. Develop a strong personal core.

Just like a house needs a foundation to support it, or as a plant needs a root system to support it, a person requires a strong personal core to support oneself. The bigger the house or plant, the stronger the foundation or root system needs to be, so if you want to grow BIG, you will require as strong a personal core as possible.

A successful life strategy requires you to take the time to ensure that your personal core is as solid as possible. Your personal core literally becomes the platform from which everything else in your life develops and grows. When your core is weak, so much of your time and energy is spent on crises control that you can't even begin to imagine leading the successful and happy life that you would like to live.

You can live with a weak personal core, constantly getting further behind rather than ahead, or you can begin building a reliable, steadfast and strong core and embark on a journey of prosperity and growth.

The choice is yours. A successful life strategy however requires a strong personal core.

Exercise: Think about all of the benefits you will reap as a result of "getting back in the driver's seat of your life" and developing a strong personal core. Describe how you want your life to be different.

Good work! Give yourself a pat on the back, look in the mirror and tell yourself "I'm Awesome!"

Tomorrow we will talk about how your comfort zone may be hindering you from getting what you want. Have a great day!

2 How Comfortable are You?

What would happen if FEAR did not influence the decisions you make? What would happen if you could move outside of your comfort zone with ease?

Many people have no idea why they stay in a place they do not like. They stay in the town they grew up in even though they do not like it. They stay in a job or career they have had for the last 15 years even though they do not find it satisfying. They stay in a bad relationship even though they do not feel happy.

They stay because they feel comfortable.

Everyone has a comfort zone. Imagine your comfort zone as a certain amount of space within you, held together with two lines on either side. For some people, the amount of space between the two lines is quite small, while for others the amount of space is much larger. Move outside of either line, and you feel "uncomfortable".

Exercise: Think of a time in your life when you really wanted something but you felt too afraid to go after it. Write about it.

_____

_____

_____

_____

_____

_____

_____

_____

_____

_____

_____

_____

_____

_____

_____

_____

_____

_____

_____

_____

_____

_____

_____

_____

The top line of your comfort zone is made up of all of the reasons you have for not going after something that you want. Even though you may really want what is beyond this line, your reasons keep you where you are.

Let's say for example, that a dream of yours is to go back to school and get your degree. You really want to get your degree. In fact, you know you could probably have a more satisfying career if you did and you know that if you don't go, down the road you will regret it.

Time goes by and you still don't go back to school. Why? You have all sorts of reasons.

- "I don't have enough money to go back to school. Tuition these days is sky high."

- "I don't have the time to go back to school. Between work and the kids, there is no way that I could find the time to fit school into my schedule."

- "I don't have the energy to go back to school. All those classes to go to and term papers to write, never mind studying for the exams. I can barely make it through the day right now."

Exercise: Make a list of some of the reasons you've used in the past to keep you from getting what you want.

_____

_____

_____

_____

_____

_____

_____

_____

_____

_____
_____
_____
_____
_____
_____
_____
_____
_____
_____
_____
_____
_____
_____
_____
_____
_____
_____
_____
_____
_____
_____
_____
_____
_____
_____
_____
_____
_____
_____

What is interesting about your comfort zone is that it doesn't matter which of the two edges you are bumping against. Fear is what keeps you from going after what you **want** above the top line of your comfort zone and fear is what keeps you from what you **don't want** below the bottom line of your comfort zone.

What you want
Top Line of your Comfort Zone

FEAR

Where you feel safe and comfortable

FEAR

Bottom Line of your Comfort Zone
What you don't want

The bottom line of your comfort zone is made up of all your reasons for not dipping below where you feel comfortable.

For example, you may think that you are the kind of person who will always have a home to go home to. In fact, when you walk by the homeless you can't imagine how they could choose to live that way. Then one day, out of the blue you get laid off - and you don't have enough savings in your bank account to cover your rent and monthly expenses.

You have dipped below the bottom edge of your comfort zone and this is where things get very uncomfortable. Naturally, you do everything in your power to either get another job or get the money you need in order to get back up where you feel safe, inside of your comfort zone.

There are two ways to view "**FEAR**":

1. "**F**_ _ _" Everything **A**nd **R**un!

Which is what most of us want to do when we feel fear.

There are times when this first definition does act in your best interest – for example, choosing not to participate in a high risk sport when you are already injured or at full capacity, or choosing to walk away from a high risk gamble where everything you have could be lost.

The majority of the time though we keep ourselves within our comfort zone for reasons that are not in our best interest, even though they appear to be.

2. **F**alse **E**vidence **A**ppearing **R**eal!

When you are smack against the top edge of your comfort zone wanting to go back to school, or asking your boss for a raise, it can feel just as scary and foolish as rock-climbing on a sheer cliff with a broken wrist or putting your life savings on what you think may be a winning hand in poker.

When you are smack against the top edge of your comfort zone the FEAR you feel is usually the result of "false evidence appearing real." You *think* you are afraid because you *believe* that something that is actually false to be true. After many years of 'believing' something, it actually can feel like it is the TRUTH, when in fact it is not. And with time you have probably found a lot of 'supporting evidence' to back up whatever false belief it is that you have.

For example, let's say that you grew up in a small town and you were taught to believe that living in a city is unsafe. You watch the news at night and read the newspaper and it is filled with evidence to confirm your belief. It becomes 'the truth' in your perspective. Then one day, you are offered a job that you have always wanted, that pays double what you are earning now – the problem is - the job is in a city. You really want to accept the job offer, but your belief that 'living in the city is unsafe' stops you from doing so.

Is your fear in this situation justified? It is true that some people living in a city have been mugged or robbed, etc. It is also true that some people have lived in a city their entire lives and have always lived safely.

The key to move beyond the top line of your comfort zone is to ask yourself what belief is holding you back, and if there truly is strong validity to support that belief.

Some of the more common false beliefs that keep people stuck inside of their comfort zone include:

- *"I am not enough"* — not good enough, smart enough, tough enough, rich enough, old enough, young enough etc.

- *"I don't deserve ......"* — because I am not loveable, not worthy, etc.

- *"Other people get ...... not me"* — because other people are better than me, my family has always been ......, I grew up in a dysfunctional family, etc.

Exercise: What are some of the beliefs that you have about yourself and the world that have kept you inside of your comfort zone?

_____

_____

_____

_____

_____

_____

_____

_____

_____

_____

There are 7 steps to challenging the beliefs that stop you from getting what you want:

1. Acknowledge that you are allowing "false beliefs" to keep you stuck inside of an imaginary comfort zone.

2. Understand that a belief is a thought that has been reinforced by experience(s) and that the feelings or emotions you have associated with that particular "false belief" do not necessarily constitute a TRUTH.

3. Understand that you often justify one belief with another and then draw from past experience(s) to make them appear even more real.

4. Ask yourself what part(s) of the belief are actually based on assumptions that you have made. List them.

5. Ask yourself if the assumption truly is "real" or if it is something that you have "made up", or was passed on to you.

6. Challenge what is not real and "reframe" the way that you think about it.

7. Start with baby steps so the process will not feel too overwhelming or else you will quickly move back to where it feels comfortable.

Exercise: Use this 7 step process to challenge 1 or 2 of the limiting beliefs that you identified.

_____

_____

_____

_____

_____

_____

Good work! Give yourself a pat on the back, look in the mirror and tell yourself "I'M AWESOME!"

Tomorrow we are going to look at how asking for what you want from other people can help you live a happier and more successful life. Have a great day!

3 | The Real Path to Safety

What would happen if you felt safe enough to BE who you really are? What would happen if the people around you didn't have to be mind readers?

Yesterday you learned how to avoid getting a false sense of security from your comfort zone.

Today you are going to learn how to develop a true sense of security that will allow you to BE fully who you are in order to get what you want.

To experience a genuine sense of inner protection that leads to healthy self-growth and expansion, you need to set strong boundaries and communicate clearly what it is you want.

Boundaries are like imaginary lines that you draw around yourself to protect you from the outside world. They literally define the way people must "be" with you and provide you with the inner sense of safety you need to be able to express who you really are.

It takes courage to get to know yourself and be willing to risk going after what you really want. Setting large boundaries therefore will give you the room you need to do so.

In this image, the inner circle represents you and the circle around you represents the space between you and the outer edge of your boundary. If the space between you and your boundary is quite small, there is not enough room for you to feel the safety you need to express who you really are.

In this image you can see that the expanded boundary gives you much more room to feel the safety you require to express who you are without getting hurt.

When you create a larger boundary you have more room in which to develop, and when you set a boundary even larger than needed, you have even more room in which to experiment and make different choices.

Exercise: Make a list of at least 3 areas where an expanded boundary would bring you a greater sense of inner safety.

_____

_____

_____

_____

_____

_____

_____

There are 4 to 6 steps to take in order to expand your boundaries.

1. Recognize where you need to set a boundary and/or an expanded boundary.

2. Define what the boundary is and then make it even larger than you think it needs to be.

3. Communicate your boundary to the person(s) involved.

4. Request that the boundary be respected.

If the boundary is not respected then:

5. Insist upon it – even if there is a possible consequence.

If it is still not respected then:

6. Follow through with the stated consequence, which may include leaving or ending the interaction with the person(s) involved.

Exercise: Go through the above 5 steps with each of the three areas you defined in the earlier.

It is important to note that boundaries are flexible (notice in the preceding images that the lines surrounding "YOU" are dashed). These 'dashed' boundaries operate in the same way as a filter, taking in what is healthy and leaving out what is harmful and unhealthy. If it were not flexible it would be like a brick wall (impermeable), not allowing anything in or out.

A boundary is set in response to a person or situation, while a wall is built as a reaction to a person or situation. Being mindful of the situation and having a strong personal core will help you to respond to people rather than react.

Boundaries (being)	Walls (doing)
Self definition	Self defense
About Me	About others/objects
About current information	About something from the past or anticipated future
You use your breath and body as a resource for information on how you are feeling	You don't check into your body – you are in your head and rational
Is a choice	Is a rule or obligation
You are being in "contact"	You are "disengaged", busy, and doing
You are personal and revealing	You are impersonal and playing a role
Your energy is alive and flexible	Your energy is rigid and inflexible
Leads to energy and passion	Leads to 'symptoms' of repression

Tips for Setting Boundaries:

- Ensure that you are not 'emotional' when you are setting a boundary. If there is emotion in your voice when you are communicating it, the message may get lost.

- Practice setting boundaries with someone with whom you feel safe.

- Use confident body language. Make sure your shoulders aren't slumping, that you are not mumbling and that you are not fidgeting.

- Use "I" statements. An "I" statement tells the listener that you are taking responsibility for your emotions and what you are saying, while a "you" statement may put the listener on the defensive.

Communicating to others the way you want them to be with you is the other way to create a healthy sense of inner safety. When the people in your life know what you expect of them, you open up a line of communication that is often left unsaid. People are not mind readers, so when you share what you require of them you are expressing yourself in a clear and respectful manner that allows them to know the conditions of the conversation. In turn, it is important that you ask the people in your life what they require of you so that you don't have to guess either.

So much pain and frustration can be avoided simply by telling people what you insist upon and what you want. If you don't, people make judgments about you, and for you, based upon their assumptions of what they "think" you want. Assumptions will always get you in trouble. Think of "assume" this way: it makes an "ass" out of "u" and "me".

Once everyone in your life knows what you expect, and you know what they expect of you, your life will be much simpler and safer.

Exercise: Do you know what you insist on in relation to the people in your life? Make a list of at least 10 things.

_____

_____

_____

_____

_____

_____

_____

_____

Exercise: Determine how you can begin to express at least 3 of these items to the people involved.

_____

_____

_____

_____

_____

_____

_____

_____

_____

_____

_____

_____

_____

_____

_____

_____

_____

_____

_____

_____

Good work! Give yourself a pat on the back, look in the mirror and tell yourself "I'M AWESOME!"

Tomorrow we are going to look at how setting higher standards can help you feel better about yourself and instantly improve the quality of your life. Have a great day!

The Path to Integrity

What would happen if you lived your life with full integrity? What would happen if you lived your life with high self-esteem?

Yesterday you learned how setting strong boundaries and communicating what you want from others can help you feel the inner safety to be who you are.

Today you are going to learn how living your life according to a set of standards that support you, will allow you to live your life with integrity, self-esteem, and fulfillment.

Personal standards refer to the actions you take in order to hold yourself accountable. When your behavior is consistent with what you stand for, you will have a greater sense of integrity and higher self-esteem than when your behavior is inconsistent with what you stand for.

For example, someone may believe in, and stand for honesty, but believes that somehow white lies won't hurt anyone. Someone else may believe in, and stand for being a law-abiding citizen, yet consistently drives over the speed limit.

Although these may appear to be rather inconsequential behaviors, they actually are not, because every time an honest person lies and a law-abiding citizen breaks the speed limit, a little piece of his or her self-esteem and integrity is torn away.

When self-esteem and integrity are torn away, self-confidence is diminished and energy is drained. If you continue living your life with these seemingly inconsequential discrepancies between what you believe in and what you stand for, your actions and your self-esteem will deteriorate and disable you from getting what you want out of life.

The first step in raising your standards is to understand what they are, right now. If you don't know what they are, then you won't know how you can raise them so that they support who you are.

To determine your standards, all you need to do is look at your behavior and what it says about the kind of person you are. (Please be loving and compassionate with yourself when you do this.) Everyone always does the best they can for what they know at any given time. When they know better, then they can do better. The worst thing you can do for your self-esteem, confidence, and energy is to start beating yourself up for the way it is now.

Exercise: Complete the following sentence at least 20 times:
"I lovingly accept that I am the kind of person who ...."

_____

_____

_____

_____

_____

_____

_____

_____

_____

_____

_____

_____

_____

_____

_____

_____

_____

_____

_____

_____

_____

_____

_____

_____

_____

_____

_____

_____

_____

_____

_____

It is also very important to remember that people's perceptions of you, are based on the standards that determine your actions in the world. How do you want people to think of you and what kind of lasting impression would you like to leave in their hearts and minds?

Legends like Mother Teresa, Martin King Jr. and Gandhi are remembered as true peacemakers and lovers of mankind. What do you think their personal standards were? Other truly great leaders of the world have left their mark in the Sciences, the Arts, and politics.

Exercise: Choose two people you admire, they may be legends in their own time, or a special neighbor who lives down the street. Make a list of 10 standards you "think" they chose to live their lives by.

_____

_____

_____

_____

_____

_____

_____

_____

_____

_____

_____

_____

_____

_____

_____

_____

_____

_____

_____

_____

_____

_____

_____

_____

_____

_____

_____

_____

_____

How would you like to be remembered? What kind of 'footprint' would you like to leave behind as a result of being born?

A good way to answer this question is to imagine that you are able to attend your own funeral. What would you like to hear other people say about you? What experience of you would you like them to have had? What lasting impressions will you have left?

Exercise: Write your own eulogy. Include how other people experienced you while you were alive and the indelible mark that you have left behind within their hearts and minds.

_____
_____
_____
_____
_____
_____
_____
_____
_____
_____
_____
_____
_____
_____
_____
_____
_____
_____
_____
_____
_____
_____
_____
_____
_____
_____
_____
_____

_____

_____

_____

_____

_____

_____

_____

_____

_____

_____

_____

_____

_____

_____

_____

_____

_____

_____

_____

_____

_____

What changes do you need to make now in order to make this vision a reality?

Exercise: Think of 5 ways that your behavior is inconsistent with what you stand for. Create 2 to 3 small action steps you could take to make it more consistent.

_____

_____

_____

_____

_____

_____

_____

_____

_____

_____

_____

_____

_____

_____

_____

_____

_____

_____

_____

_____

_____

Good work! Give yourself a pat on the back, look in the mirror and tell yourself "I'M AWESOME!"

Tomorrow we are going to look at how you can begin to focus on what is truly important to you by getting your personal needs met on a consistent basis. Have a great day!

Who Really is in Control?

What would happen if you were able to get all of your needs met in a constructive and consistent manner? What would happen if you could focus on what is truly important to you rather than on what you "think" is important?

Yesterday you learned how ensuring that your actions are in alignment with your true self can boost your self-confidence, self-esteem, and integrity.

Today you are going to learn how getting your needs met in a beneficial way can do the same.

On Day 1 you read about the many people who live their lives on autopilot, living from one day to the next, often oblivious to what is motivating their behavior. If they took the time to reflect on how they are choosing to live their lives, they would discover that most of their time and energy has been spent chasing after unfulfilled needs.

We all have needs. Some are universal (like food, water, air, shelter, love) and some are unique to each individual. Some of the unique needs you have are quite obvious to you, while other needs are so obscure that they are literally unconscious. Unique needs include experiences like: control, attention, approval, recognition, admiration, autonomy, intensity, and superiority, quiet and respite. The need in and of itself is neither positive or negative, it just is.

Although you have two types of needs, your ego cannot distinguish the difference between them. To your ego, the need for recognition, for example, is just as important as the need for air and it will do everything in its power to get it fulfilled (be it consciously identified or not).

Your unique needs were acquired from the needs that were unfulfilled during the formative years of your life and as a result they are literally like having holes inside of you that have to be filled. Because they are so important to your ego, you may have been putting a vast amount of your time and energy, even though you don't realize it, into getting these needs met.

Your ego does not care how you get your needs fulfilled. As a result you may be getting them met in ways that are good for you, ways that are not good for you, or a combination of both.

For example, a person with a need for attention may get it met constructively by being an entertainer who is consistently in the limelight, or destructively by getting drunk and making a scene. Both scenarios bring attention to the person.

Exercise: Think of 3 obvious unique needs that you have. List at least 2 or 3 ways that you have attempted to meet them both constructively and destructively in the past.

_____

_____

_____

_____

_____

_____

_____

_____

_____

_____

_____

_____

_____

_____

_____

_____

_____

_____

_____

_____

_____

_____

_____

_____

_____

Your personal needs may mask what you truly deem important and as a result you may spend a lot of time and energy chasing after what you think is most important, when in fact it is not.

Ways to Get your Needs Met:

1. Identify the needs that are driving you.

As noted earlier, some needs are more obvious than others. Start by listing the ones that strongly come to mind. Next, make a timeline of your life, listing events that you are particularly displeased with or ashamed of (it is generally easier for your ego to get a need met destructively). Contemplate experiences in your life and perhaps even write out your life story. Look for any patterns that pop up. Pay particular attention to the needs that you really don't like, because some of your more obscure needs may be needs you are unnecessarily embarrassed of.

• **Make a list of the needs that strongly come to mind right now.**

_____

_____

_____

_____

_____

_____

_____

_____

_____

_____

_____

- **Make a timeline of your life, listing the events you are not proud of.**

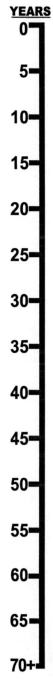

• **Make a list of any patterns that you see.**

_____

_____

_____

_____

_____

_____

_____

_____

_____

_____

_____

2. Prioritize the list of needs you came up with.

Narrow your list down to 3 to 5 needs that you want to begin working on right away.

_____

_____

_____

_____

_____

_____

3. Develop a proactive plan for getting your needs met consistently in a constructive manner.

Think of simple ways to this. For example, a person may get their need for control met simply by adhering to a regular routine.

---

4. Improve your self-care.

Healthy forms of energy like good food, exercise and sufficient rest will help you to avoid charging yourself with the adrenaline brought out by unmet needs. Think of some ways that you can improve your self-care.

---

5. Stop Blaming Others.

It does not matter where you acquired a certain need. Accept the responsibility for getting your needs met. Accept that you have these needs and deal with them appropriately. Explain how you will do this.

_____

_____

_____

_____

_____

_____

_____

_____

_____

_____

_____

Once you have control of your needs you will have the time and energy to devote to what is really most important – your core values.

Good work! Give yourself a pat on the back, look in the mirror and tell yourself "I'M AWESOME!"

Tomorrow we are going to see how defining and living your life according to your values is the key to fulfillment and success. Have a great day!

6 Living from the Inside-Out

What would happen if you had a guaranteed method to determine if the decisions you are making and/or the goals you are setting are right for you?

What would happen if you could determine what you are most passionate about and had a way to systematically apply these passions to your life?

Yesterday you learned how understanding your needs and then finding ways of getting them met in a consistent and constructive manner can make room for what is truly important in your life. Today you are going to learn how to determine what is most important to you, so that the majority of your time and energy can be spent experiencing it.

Many people live a DO – HAVE – BE lifestyle – which is living from the 'outside-in'. They *Do* all sorts of things in order to *Have* the things they think they need in order to *Be* happy. Over the short term this is an acceptable way of living. Over the long term however it is unsustainable.

Material objects can only bring so much happiness. Having "things" is not bad – but they are not going to bring you the deep inner satisfaction we all long for.

In order to live a life that brings a true sense of meaning, purpose, and deep fulfillment you need to live a BE – DO – HAVE lifestyle, or in other words, live from the 'inside-out'. Living this kind of life requires you to *Be*, to reflect upon what is most important to you and what it is that brings you the greatest sense of passion. Then you *Do* those things in order to *Have* those experiences.

When you are living your life from the inside-out, your life becomes much simpler. You will intuitively know how you want to spend your time and you will not be distracted by what is not important to you. When you are living from the outside-in, your life is complex. You will be constantly distracted by what is not important to you because you will be constantly searching for something to make you happy.

Making decisions and setting goals becomes very easy once you ask yourself if what you are thinking about is in alignment with what is most important to you. If it is important – great, then you can go ahead with it. If it isn't – that is great too, because you will not have wasted your time and energy.

What is most important to you comes from the core of your being. These core values are most important to you because they express who you really are. When acting out your core values you feel most alive, energized and at one with the universe. Many people report that when they are doing an activity they are very passionate about, time literally appears to stand still.

*** Note that the needs you are getting fulfilled destructively can give you a false sense of energy through the adrenaline they produce. It is important to not confuse these false energies with the deep sense of fulfillment and energy you experience when you are living from the inside-out.

Exercise: List as many experiences as you can remember when you have felt most alive, energized, at one with the universe – when time seemed to stand still.

_____

_____

_____

_____

_____

_____

_____

_____

_____

_____

_____

_____

_____

_____

_____

_____

_____

_____

_____

_____

_____

_____

Exercise: Ask yourself what exactly it is about those particular experiences that allowed you to feel that way.

_____

_____

_____

_____

_____

_____

_____

_____

_____

_____

_____

_____

_____

_____

_____

_____

_____

_____

_____

_____

_____

_____

_____

You may be having difficulty thinking of times when you have experienced the deep level of fulfillment that living from the inside-out can bring. This difficulty may be due to a sense of having spent so much of your life chasing after needs, putting everyone and everything ahead of you and making your decisions based on feelings of obligation and duty. Long periods of excessive stress, tolerating difficulties, handling money problems and varying addictions can also hinder your ability to tap into what is most important to you.

If this is true for you, not to worry, because as you begin to strengthen the other parts of your personal core (boundaries, standards and needs) your innermost desires and dreams will begin to surface and be revealed. In addition, there are other steps that you can take to uncover what you are truly passionate about.

Ways to Get in Touch with what is Important to You:

1. Construct a timeline of your life, making note of the times that you have felt the proudest of yourself, the most alive and the most passionate.

Ask yourself what it was that you were experiencing that caused you to feel that way. Chances are you will begin to see a pattern develop.

• Construct a timeline of your life listing events when you have felt most alive.

YEARS

• **List any patterns that you see.**

_____

_____

_____

_____

_____

_____

_____

_____

_____

2. Go back into your childhood and ask yourself what you liked to spend your time doing.

Then ask yourself what kind of feelings you experienced in those moments that caused you to want to spend your time in that way.

_____

_____

_____

_____

_____

_____

_____

_____

_____

_____

_____

3. Take a look at the list of people you most admire (Day 4), and write a comparison of the qualities you admire that these people possess in relation to your own.

Check for patterns – the reason you admire them is because they are reflections of what you value most.

_____

_____

_____

_____

_____

_____

_____

_____

_____

_____

Now that you have started to get an idea of your values, it is important that you begin taking steps to ensure that you experience them more often.

Steps to Living your life from the Inside-Out:

1. Choose 2 or 3 things that are important to you and find some very simple ways of getting them met.

For example if beauty is very important to you, surrounding yourself with beautiful things in your home, going to the museum or going for walks in nature could be some simple ways to experience the value of beauty on a regular basis. If learning is important to you, reading informative books, watching educational programs on TV or taking a course at your local community college could be simple ways to experience the value of learning on a regular basis. If adventure is important to you, finding several new routes to drive to work, exploring a new neighborhood in your city or reading books filled with suspense and intrigue could be simple ways to experience the value of adventure on a regular basis. You get the picture.

---

2. Generate more ideas of activities to ensure that you are experiencing what is important to you on a continuous basis.

For some people this step may require you to reprioritize different aspects of your life, while for others it may require you to make significant changes in your behavior.

_____

_____

_____

_____

_____

_____

_____

_____

_____

_____

_____

_____

_____

3. Whenever you are faced with a decision to make or a goal to set, ask yourself if what you are thinking about is in alignment with what is most important to you.

Only choose to do those things that are in alignment with your passions because when you do, you will be choosing to live with integrity.

Good work! Give yourself a pat on the back, look in the mirror and tell yourself "I'M AWESOME!"

You have now completed all of the sections on strengthening your personal core. Tomorrow you are going to look at all of the various elements that make "you" YOU and what your current level of satisfaction is in those areas. Have a great day!

Your Starting Point

I f you always do what you have always done, then you will always get what you've always got. Once you do something different, you will get something different. Therefore the second secret to creating your ultimate life is to have a clear understanding of what you are doing now, so you will know what it is you need to do differently.

On days 7 through 12 you will develop a clear picture of what your life is like in 8 specific areas. These areas include: your career, your relationship with friends and family, your relationship with your significant partner, your fun and recreation, your health, your personal growth, your finances and your personal environment. During these 6 days of the Bootcamp you will clearly discern what you like and don't like, what works and doesn't, and what you have and don't have in each of these 8 areas. By the end of Day 12 you will know what you need to do differently.

7 The Elements of your Life

What would happen if you knew exactly what was working in your life? What would happen if you knew exactly what wasn't working in your life?

Over the past few days you have been learning about the importance of creating a life strategy and how a strong personal core and expanded comfort zone can help you.

Today you are going learn the importance of having a clear understanding of what your life is like right now.

If you live in Chicago and you want to go to New York, you are not going to get anywhere if you plan your trip from Los Angeles. The same is true for your life. You need to know exactly where you are right now, in order to get to where it is you want to go. You need to know what it is like right now, in order to know how you want it to be in the future. The present is your only possible starting point.

Exercise: Rate your current level of satisfaction with your life in general on a scale of 1 to 10 (with 1 being the lowest and 10 being the highest).

My current level of satisfaction with my life is:

_____.

The "Elements of Your Life" diagram below characterizes many different aspects of your life. Please look at each element, and rate what your current level of satisfaction with each aspect is on a scale of 1 to 10 (with 1 being the least satisfied and 10 being the most satisfied).

You will notice that there are some areas of your life that you feel better about than others. It is natural for your scores to vary (even considerably).

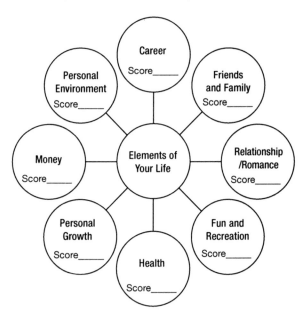

In each area, regardless of its score, there will be parts of your life that are working well for you and parts that are not. Gaining awareness of both can help you to increase your successes and decrease your disappointments.

Exercise: Write down at least 3 to 5 things that are working well in each of these areas of your life.

Career:_____

_____

_____

_____

_____

_____

Friends and Family:_____

_____

_____

_____

_____

Relationship/Romance:_____

_____

_____

_____

_____

Fun and Recreation:_____

_____

_____

_____

_____

Health:_____

_____

_____

_____

_____

_____

Personal Growth:_____

_____

_____

_____

_____

Money:_____

_____

_____

_____

_____

Personal Environment:_____

_____

_____

_____

_____

Exercise: Write down at least 3 to 5 things that are not working well in each of these areas of your life.

Career:_____

_____

_____

_____

_____

_____

Friends and Family:_____

_____

_____

_____

_____

Relationship/Romance:_____

_____

_____

_____

_____

Fun and Recreation:_____

_____

_____

_____

_____

Health:_____

_____

_____

_____

_____

_____

Personal Growth:_____

_____

_____

_____

_____

Money:_____

_____

_____

_____

_____

Personal Environment:_____

_____

_____

_____

_____

Good work! Give yourself a pat on the back, look in the mirror and tell yourself "I'M AWESOME!"

Tomorrow you are going to apply what you learned about the differences between false and true "beliefs" to each area of the "Elements of Your Life" diagram. Have a great day!

8 | Know what you Believe

What would happen if you knew what your beliefs were in each area of your life? What would happen if you could reframe your limiting beliefs; the ones that propel you forward?

On Day 2 you learned how staying within your comfort zone can keep you from living the life you want.

Today you are going to apply what you have learned about reframing limiting beliefs to the different areas within the "Elements of your Life" diagram. For each area, you are going to write down 10 beliefs and then challenge 3 to 5 of them by using the reframing technique taught in Day 2.

Let's go over the reframing technique again in order to refresh your memory.

There are 7 steps to challenging the beliefs that stop you from getting what you want:

1. Acknowledge that you are allowing "false beliefs" to keep you stuck inside of an imaginary and restrictive comfort zone.

2. Understand that a belief is a thought that has been reinforced by experience(s) and that the feelings or emotions you have associated with that particular "false belief" do not necessarily constitute a TRUTH.

3. Understand that you often justify one belief with another and then draw from past experience(s) to make them appear even more real.

4. Ask yourself what part(s) of the belief are actually based on assumptions that you have made. List them.

5. Ask yourself if the assumption is truly "real" or if it is something that you have "made up" or has been passed on to you.

6. Challenge what is not real and "reframe" the way that you think about it.

7. Start with baby steps so the process will not feel too overwhelming (or else you will quickly move back to your restricted comfort zone).

Exercise: Write 10 beliefs that you have in the area of Career from the "Elements of your Life" diagram.

_____

_____

_____

_____

_____

_____

_____

_____

_____

Exercise: Challenge 3-5 of these beliefs by using the re-framing technique taught to you in Day 2:

_____

_____

_____

_____

_____

Exercise: Write 10 beliefs that you have in the area of Family and Friends from the "Elements of your Life" diagram.

_____

_____

_____

_____

_____

_____

_____

_____

_____

_____

Exercise: Challenge 3-5 of these beliefs by using the re-framing technique taught to you in Day 2:

_____

_____

_____

_____

_____

Exercise: Write 10 beliefs that you have in the area of Relationship/Romance from the "Elements of your Life" diagram.

_____

_____

_____

_____

_____

_____

_____

_____

_____

Exercise: Challenge 3-5 of these beliefs by using the re-framing technique taught to you in Day 2:

_____

_____

_____

_____

Exercise: Write 10 beliefs that you have in the area of Fun and Recreation from the "Elements of your Life" diagram.

_____

_____

_____

_____

_____

_____

_____

_____

_____

_____

Exercise: Challenge 3-5 of these beliefs by using the re-framing technique taught to you in Day 2:

_____

_____

_____

_____

Exercise: Write 10 beliefs that you have in the area of Health from the "Elements of your Life" diagram.

_____

_____

_____

_____

_____

_____

_____

_____

_____

_____

Exercise: Challenge 3-5 of these beliefs by using the re-framing technique taught to you in Day 2:

_____

_____

_____

_____

_____

Exercise: Write 10 beliefs that you have in the area of Money from the "Elements of your Life" diagram.

_____

_____

_____

_____

_____

_____

_____

_____

_____

_____

Exercise: Challenge 3-5 of these beliefs by using the re-framing technique taught to you in Day 2:

_____

_____

_____

_____

_____

Exercise: Write 10 beliefs that you have in the area of Personal Growth from the "Elements of your Life" diagram.

_____

_____

_____

_____

_____

_____

_____

_____

_____

_____

Exercise: Challenge 3-5 of these beliefs by using the re-framing technique taught to you in Day 2:

_____

_____

_____

_____

_____

Exercise: Write 10 beliefs that you have in the area of Physical Environment from the "Elements of your Life" diagram.

_____

_____

_____

_____

Exercise: Challenge 3-5 of these beliefs by using the re-framing technique taught to you in Day 2:

Good work! Give yourself a pat on the back, look in the mirror and tell yourself "I'M AWESOME!"

Tomorrow you are going to apply what you have learned about setting boundaries and effectively communicating what you want, to every element of your life.

Know what you Want

What would happen if you knew what your boundaries were in each area of your life? What would happen if people behaved the way you want them to in every area of your life?

On Day-3 you learned that a true sense of inner safety comes as a result of setting large boundaries and communicating to people the way you want them to behave around you.

Today you are going to apply what you have learned about these two areas of your personal core to the different areas within the "Elements of your Life" diagram. For each area, you are going to be asked to write down 10 boundaries and/or ways you want people to behave around you, and then choose 3 to 5 of them that you will communicate and change within three months.

Let's go over the steps for setting and expanding your boundaries again in order to refresh your memory.

1. Recognize where you need to set a boundary or a larger one.

2. Define what the boundary is and then make it three times larger than you think it needs to be.

3. Communicate your boundary to the person(s) involved.

4. Request that the boundary be respected.

If the boundary is not respected then:

5. Insist upon it with even a possible consequence.

If it is still not respected then:

6. Follow-through with the stated consequence, which may include leaving or ending the interaction with person(s) involved.

Exercise: Write 10 boundaries and/or ways you want people to behave around you in the area of Career from the "Elements of your Life" diagram.

_____

_____

_____

_____

_____

_____

_____

_____

_____

_____

Exercise: Choose 3 to 5 of the above that you will communicate within three months:

_____
_____
_____
_____
_____

Exercise: Write 10 boundaries and/or ways you want people to behave around you in the area of Family and Friends from the "Elements of your Life" diagram.

_____
_____
_____
_____
_____
_____
_____
_____
_____
_____

Exercise: Choose 3 to 5 of the above that you will communicate within three months:

_____
_____
_____
_____
_____

Exercise: Write 10 boundaries and/or ways you want people to behave around you in the area of Relationship/Romance from the "Elements of your Life" diagram.

_____

_____

_____

_____

_____

_____

_____

_____

_____

_____

Exercise: Choose 3 to 5 of the above that you will communicate within three months:

_____

_____

_____

_____

Exercise: Write 10 boundaries and/or ways you want people to behave around you in the area of Fun and Recreation from the "Elements of your Life" diagram.

_____

_____

_____

_____

_____

_____

_____

_____

_____

_____

Exercise: Choose 3 to 5 of the above that you will communicate within three months:

_____

_____

_____

_____

_____

Exercise: Write 10 boundaries and/or ways you want people to behave around you in the area of Health from the "Elements of your Life" diagram.

_____

_____

_____

_____

_____

_____

_____

_____

_____

Exercise: Choose 3 to 5 of the above that you will communicate within three months:

_____

_____

_____

_____

_____

Exercise: Write 10 boundaries and/or ways you want people to behave around you in the area of Money from the "Elements of your life" diagram.

_____

_____

_____

_____

_____

_____

_____

_____

_____

_____

Exercise: Choose 3 to 5 of the above that you will communicate within three months:

_____

_____

_____

_____

_____

Exercise: Write 10 boundaries and/or ways you want people to behave around you in the area of Personal Growth from the "Elements of your Life" diagram.

_____

_____

_____

_____

_____

_____

_____

_____

_____

_____

Exercise: Choose 3 to 5 of the above that you will communicate within three months:

_____

_____

_____

_____

_____

Exercise: Write 10 boundaries and/or ways you want people to behave around you in the area of Physical Environment from the "Elements of your Life" diagram.

_____

_____

Exercise: Choose 3 to 5 of the above that you will communicate within three months:

Good work! Give yourself a pat on the back, look in the mirror and tell yourself "I'M AWESOME!"

Tomorrow you are going to apply what you learned about setting standards to every element of your life. Have a great day!

Know what you Stand For

What would happen if you knew what you stood for in every area of your life? What would happen if your behavior was consistently in integrity with who you really are?

On Day 4 you learned that raising your standards puts your choices and decisions in greater alignment with who you really are. As a result, your behavior supports your true self, and your self-esteem, confidence, and integrity, all immediately increase.

Today you are going to apply what you have learned about standards to the elements of your life that we have been working with. For each area, you are going to be asked to write down 10 standards that you have, and then to choose 3 to 5 of them that you can upgrade immediately.

Let's go over the steps for raising your standards again to refresh your memory.

The first step in aligning your behavior with what you stand for is to understand where your behavior is right now. Being loving and compassionate with yourself when you do this is very important. You cannot raise your self-esteem and confidence if you are beating yourself up for what you are currently doing.

The second step is to design action steps to immediately upgrade your behavior. For example, if you are the kind of person who consistently speeds even though you consider yourself to be a "law-abiding citizen," you can immediately upgrade your behavior by simply deciding to keep to the speed limit. When you are driving on the highway you can set the cruise control to make it even easier. During this process you need to remember that you are replacing one habit for another and that it takes at least 21 times of doing the new habit for it to sink in.

Exercise: Write 10 behaviors that are inconsistent with what you stand for in the area of Career from the "Elements of your Life" diagram.

_____

_____

_____

_____

_____

_____

_____

_____

_____

_____

Exercise: Choose 3 to 5 behaviors to be upgraded immediately:

_____

_____

_____

_____

_____

Exercise: Write 10 behaviors that are inconsistent with what you stand for in the area of Family and Friends from the "Elements of your Life" diagram.

_____

_____

_____

_____

_____

_____

_____

_____

_____

_____

Exercise: Choose 3 to 5 behaviors to be upgraded immediately:

_____

_____

_____

_____

_____

Exercise: Write 10 behaviors that are inconsistent with what you stand for in the area of Relationship/ Romance from the "Elements of your Life" diagram.

_____

_____

_____

_____

_____

_____

_____

_____

_____

Exercise: Choose 3 to 5 behaviors to be upgraded immediately:

_____

_____

_____

_____

Exercise: Write 10 behaviors that are inconsistent with what you stand for in the area of Fun and Recreation from the "Elements of your Life" diagram.

_____

_____

_____

_____

_____

_____

_____

_____

_____

_____

_____

Exercise: Choose 3 to 5 behaviors to be upgraded immediately:

_____

_____

_____

_____

_____

Exercise: Write 10 behaviors that are inconsistent with what you stand for in the area of Health from the "Elements of your Life" diagram.

_____

_____

_____

_____

_____

_____

_____

_____

_____

_____

Exercise: Choose 3 to 5 behaviors to be upgraded immediately:

_____

_____

_____

_____

_____

Exercise: Write 10 behaviors that are inconsistent with what you stand for in the area of Money from the "Elements of your Life" diagram.

_____

_____

_____

_____

_____

_____

_____

_____

_____

_____

Exercise: Choose 3 to 5 behaviors to be upgraded immediately:

_____

_____

_____

_____

_____

Exercise: Write 10 behaviors that are inconsistent with what you stand for in the area of Personal Growth from the "Elements of your Life" diagram.

_____

_____

_____

_____

_____

_____

_____

_____

_____

_____

Exercise: Choose 3 to 5 behaviors to be upgraded immediately:

_____

_____

_____

_____

_____

Exercise: Write 10 behaviors that are inconsistent with what you stand for in the area of Physical Environment from the "Elements of your Life" diagram.

_____

_____

_____

_____

_____

_____

_____

_____

_____

_____

Exercise: Choose 3 to 5 behaviors to be upgraded immediately:

_____

_____

_____

_____

_____

Good work! Give yourself a pat on the back, look in the mirror and tell yourself "I'M AWESOME!"

Tomorrow you are going to apply what you learned about evaluating your needs to every element of your life. Have a great day!

Know what you Need

What would happen if you consistently and constructively fulfilled all of your needs in every area of your life? What would happen if you stopped chasing after your needs and began focusing on what you really want?

On Day 5 you learned that we all have needs that MUST be met and that learning to do so in a consistently constructive way can free up your time and energy to experience what really matters to you.

You will remember that having needs is not the same as being needy. In fact, expressing your needs and asking others to help you fulfill them, is behaving responsibly and with accountably. Needs are nothing to be embarrassed about – they just "are". Resisting or denying the needs that you don't like will just set you up for some form of self-sabotage down the road because your ego will INSIST that they be met (usually destructively).

Today you are going to apply what you have learned about needs to the elements of your life that we have been working with over the past few days. For each area, you are going to be asked to write down 10 needs that you think you have and then to come up with at least one way to get 3 to 5 of them met in a consistent and constructive manner.

Let's go over the steps for getting your needs met in order to refresh your memory.

Ways to Get your Needs Met:

1. Identify the unique needs that you have. As noted earlier some needs are more obvious than others.

2. Prioritize the list of needs. Narrow your list down to 5 that you want to begin working on right away.

3. Develop a proactive plan to getting them met consistently in a constructive manner.

4. Choose Positive Sources of Energy.

5. Stop Blaming Others. It does not matter where you acquired a certain need and it is up to you to take full responsibility for getting them met.

Exercise: Write 10 needs that you have in the area of Career from the "Elements of your Life" diagram.

_____

_____

_____

_____

_____

_____

_____

_____

_____

_____

Exercise: Choose 3 to 5 of these needs and write down at least one way that you can begin to get them met in a consistent and constructive manner.

_____

_____

_____

_____

_____

Exercise: Write 10 needs that you have in the area of Family and Friends from the "Elements of your Life" diagram.

_____

_____

_____

_____

_____

_____

_____

_____

_____

_____

Exercise: Choose 3 to 5 of these needs and write down at least one way that you can begin to get them met in a consistent and constructive manner.

_____

_____

_____

_____

_____

_____

Exercise: Write 10 needs that you have in the area of Relationship/Romance from the "Elements of your Life" diagram.

_____

_____

_____

_____

_____

_____

_____

_____

_____

_____

Exercise: Choose 3 to 5 of these needs and write down at least one way that you can begin to get them met in a consistent and constructive manner.

_____

_____

_____

_____

_____

Exercise: Write 10 needs that you have in the area of Fun and Recreation from the "Elements of your Life" diagram.

_____

_____

_____

_____

_____

_____

_____

_____

_____

_____

Exercise: Choose 3 to 5 of these needs and write down at least one way that you can begin to get them met in a consistent and constructive manner.

_____

_____

_____

_____

_____

Exercise: Write 10 needs that you have in the area of Health from the "Elements of your Life" diagram.

_____

_____

_____

_____

_____

_____

_____

_____

_____

_____

_____

Exercise: Choose 3 to 5 of these needs and write down at least one way that you can begin to get them met in a consistent and constructive manner.

_____

_____

_____

_____

Exercise: Write 10 needs that you have in the area of Money from the "Elements of your Life" diagram.

_____

_____

_____

_____

_____

_____

_____

_____

_____

_____

Exercise: Choose 3 to 5 of these needs and write down at least one way that you can begin to get them met in a consistent and constructive manner.

Exercise: Write 10 needs that you have in the area of Personal Growth from the "Elements of your Life" diagram.

Exercise: Choose 3 to 5 of these needs and write down at least one way that you can begin to get them met in a consistent and constructive manner.

Exercise: Write 10 needs that you have in the area of Physical Environment from the "Elements of your Life" diagram.

_____

_____

_____

_____

_____

_____

_____

_____

_____

Exercise: Choose 3 to 5 of these needs and write down at least one way that you can begin to get them met in a consistent and constructive manner.

_____

_____

_____

_____

_____

Good work! Give yourself a pat on the back, look in the mirror and tell yourself "I'M AWESOME!"

Tomorrow you are going to apply what you learned about living from the "inside-out" to every element of your life. Have a great day!

Know what is Important to You

What would happen if you knew what was most important to you? What would happen if you focused only on what is most important to you in every element of your life?

On Day 6, you learned the most efficient way of living a successful and rewarding life is to live from the 'inside-out'. Living this kind of life requires you to Be, to reflect upon what is most important to you and what brings you the greatest sense of passion. You Do those things in order to Have those experiences. Determining what is most important to you in every area of your life will help you to live a complete 'inside-out' lifestyle.

Today you are going to apply the 'inside-out' principle to the various elements of your life. For each element, you are going to be asked to write down 10 things that are important to you, and to write down one way to get 3 to 5 of these fulfilled in a very simple way.

To refresh your memory, let's go over the steps to determine what is most important to you.

Steps to living from the inside-out:

1. List as many experiences you can remember when you have felt most alive, energized, at one with the universe – when time seemed to stand still.

2. Ask yourself what exactly it is about those particular experiences that allowed you to feel that way.

3. Choose 2 or 3 things that are important to you and find some very simple ways of getting these values met.

4. Generate ideas about different kinds of activities. Since some activities may take time to implement, having multiple activities that take varying lengths of time will ensure you are experiencing what is important to you on a continuous basis.

5. Whenever you are faced with a decision to make or a goal to set, ask yourself if what you are thinking about is in alignment with what is most important to you.

Exercise: Write 10 things that are important to you in the area of Career from the "Elements of your Life" diagram.

_____

_____

_____

_____

_____

_____

_____

_____

_____

_____

Exercise: Choose one way to get 3 to 5 of these fulfilled in a very simple way:

_____

_____

_____

_____

_____

Exercise: Write 10 things that are important to you in the area of Family and Friends from the "Elements of your Life" diagram.

_____

_____

_____

_____

_____

_____

_____

_____

_____

_____

Exercise: Choose one way to get 3 to 5 of these fulfilled in a very simple way:

_____

_____

_____

_____

_____

Exercise: Write 10 things that are important to you in the area of Relationship/Romance from the "Elements of your Life" diagram.

_____

_____

_____

_____

_____

_____

_____

_____

_____

_____

Exercise: Choose one way to get 3 to 5 of these fulfilled in a very simple way:

_____

_____

_____

_____

Exercise: Write 10 things that are important to you in the area of Fun and Recreation from the "Elements of your Life" diagram.

_____

_____

_____

_____

_____
_____
_____
_____
_____
_____

Exercise: Choose one way to get 3 to 5 of these fulfilled in a very simple way:

_____
_____
_____
_____
_____

Exercise: Write 10 things that are important to you in the area of Health from the "Elements of your Life" diagram.

_____
_____
_____
_____
_____
_____
_____
_____
_____
_____

Exercise: Choose one way to get 3 to 5 of these fulfilled in a very simple way:

_____

_____

_____

_____

_____

Exercise: Write 10 things that are important to you in the area of Money from the "Elements of your Life" diagram.

_____

_____

_____

_____

_____

_____

_____

_____

_____

_____

Exercise: Choose one way to get 3 to 5 of these fulfilled in a very simple way:

_____

_____

_____

_____

_____

Exercise: Write 10 things that are important to you in the area of Personal Growth from the "Elements of your Life" diagram.

_____

_____

_____

_____

_____

_____

_____

_____

_____

Exercise: Choose one way to get 3 to 5 of these fulfilled in a very simple way:

_____

_____

_____

_____

_____

Exercise: Write 10 things that are important to you in the area of Physical Environment from the "Elements of your Life" diagram.

_____

_____

_____

_____

_____

_____

_____

_____

_____

_____

Exercise: Choose one way to get 3 to 5 of these fulfilled in a very simple way:

_____

_____

_____

_____

_____

Good work! Give yourself a pat on the back, look in the mirror and tell yourself "I'M AWESOME!"

You have now finished applying what you have learned about your personal core to each area of the "Elements of your Life" diagram. Tomorrow you are going to learn about the importance of creating an inspiring and compelling vision for the future. Have a great day!

Your Ultimate Destination

A successful journey has a definite starting and end point. Now that you know where you have been it is time for you to determine where you will go. Therefore the third secret to creating your ultimate life is to have a clear vision of what your life could be.

On days 13 to 21 you will define compelling and motivating visions for your future that will give you the fortitude and momentum you need to create the life of your dreams. This is where the heat gets turned up, and you begin to move full throttle towards what could be, and what you could be experiencing in every area of your life.

What is your Vision of the Future?

W hat would happen if you had a compelling and motivating vision for the future? What would happen if it were to come true?

Now that you have a good understanding of your personal core and how its components need to be implemented into each element of your life, it is time to begin imagining what is possible for your future.

On Day 7 you learned how important it is to understand where you are 'right now' in order to create what you want. Today you are going to learn how important it is to know 'where you are going' in order to create what you want.

You learned that if you live in Chicago and you want to go to New York that you are not going to get anywhere if you plan your trip from Los Angeles. The same holds true if you live in Chicago, and you want to go to New York, and you plan your trip to Miami instead. If you follow this plan, you will end up in Miami and not in New York, which is not at all what you wanted.

There are different ways that you can determine what you want to experience in your future. Today you are going to use three different exercises to help you decide how you want your future to be.

1. Reread your work from yesterday, as well Day 6, about everything that is most important to you.

2. Make a list of 50 things you want to experience during your lifetime.

3. Write a letter to yourself as your future self (aged 90) and describe the "past" experiences in your life that have brought you the most pride and joy.

Each of these exercises is designed to view your possible future from a different perspective. Looking ahead from where you are right now, at the life you want to create, is a very useful way of looking at the future. Imagining yourself at a future age and then looking back at your life and what brought you the most satisfaction will give you another point of view to reflect upon. Each one is just as valid as the next.

So, have fun with these exercises and pay close attention to what comes up!

Exercise: Reread the work you did on Days 6 and 12, and make a list of things you found important.

_____

_____

_____

_____

_____

_____

_____

_____

_____

_____

_____

_____

_____

_____

_____

_____

_____

_____

_____

_____

_____

_____

_____

_____

_____

_____

_____

_____

_____

_____

_____

_____

_____

_____

_____

Exercise: Make a list of 50 things that you want to experience in your lifetime.

_____

_____

_____

_____

_____

_____

_____

_____

_____

_____

_____

_____

_____

_____

_____

_____

_____

_____

_____

_____

_____

_____

_____

_____

_____

_____

_____

_____

_____

_____

_____

_____

_____

_____

_____

_____

_____

_____

_____

_____

_____

_____

_____

_____

Exercise: Write a letter to yourself as your 'future self at aged 90' and describe the experiences that have brought you pride and joy in your life. To help you get inside of your 'role,' use your non-dominant hand to write the letter.

Good work! Give yourself a pat on the back, look in the mirror and tell yourself "I'M AWESOME!"

Tomorrow you are going to apply what you learned about envisioning a terrific future to the various elements of your life. Have a great day!

Long Term Vision of your Career

W hat would happen if you had an inspiring and compelling vision for your career? What would happen if you were to get so clear about the way you want your career to be that you could practically taste it?

Yesterday you learned why it is so important to create a long term vision of what you want.

Today you are going to apply what you have learned to your career. You are going to write a long term vision for how you want your career to be 6 months from now, a year from now, 5 years from now, and 10 years from now. You are going to begin with the "end in mind" so you will know what it is you are ultimately aiming for with each career vision you write.

Please include as many concrete examples in your visions as possible in order to make them appear to be real. Include: what you see when you are working, what you hear other people say while at work, how you feel when you are at work and what you are doing at work.

The more detailed your career visions are, the greater the chance you have of bringing your visions to fruition.

Have fun!

Exercise: Write a detailed long term vision for how you would like your career to be 10 years from now.

_____

_____

_____

_____

_____

_____

_____

_____

_____

_____

_____

_____

_____

_____

_____

_____

_____

_____

_____

_____

Exercise: Write a detailed long term vision for how you would like your career to be 5 years from now.

_____

_____

_____

_____

_____

_____

_____

_____

_____

_____

_____

_____

_____

_____

_____

_____

_____

_____

_____

_____

_____

_____

Exercise: Write a detailed long term vision for how you would like your career to be 1 year from now.

Exercise: Write a detailed long term vision for how you would like your career to be 6 months from now.

_____

_____

_____

_____

_____

_____

_____

_____

_____

_____

_____

_____

_____

_____

_____

_____

_____

_____

Good work! Give yourself a pat on the back, look in the mirror and tell yourself "I'M AWESOME!"

Tomorrow you are going write long term visions for the area of "family and friends! Have a great day!

Long Term Vision of your Family and Friends

hat would happen if you had an inspiring and compelling vision for your relationships with family and friends? What would happen if you were to get so clear about the way you want that area of your life to be that you could practically taste it?

Yesterday you applied what you have learned about long term visions to the area of your career.

Today you are going to be applying similar strategies to the area of "family and friends." You are going to write a long term vision for how you want your social sphere to be 6 months from now, a year from now, 5 years from now and 10 years from now. You are going to begin with the "end in mind" so you will know what kinds of social relationships you are ultimately aiming for with each vision your write.

Remember to include concrete examples in your visions. Include: what you see in your future social relationships, what you hear other people say when you are around them, how you feel when you are with them and what you are doing with them. The more detailed your visions of your social sphere are, the greater the chance you have of manifesting these visions in your social life.

Have fun!

> **Exercise:** Write a detailed long term vision for how you would like the area of family and friends to be 10 years from now.

_____

_____

_____

_____

_____

_____

_____

_____

_____

_____

_____

_____

_____

_____

_____

_____

_____

_____

Exercise: Write a detailed long term vision for how you would like the area of family and friends to be 5 years from now.

_____

_____

_____

_____

_____

_____

_____

_____

_____

_____

_____

_____

_____

_____

_____

_____

_____

_____

_____

_____

_____

Exercise: Write a detailed long term vision for how you would like the area of family and friends to be 1 year from now.

_____

_____

_____

_____

_____

_____

_____

_____

_____

_____

_____

_____

_____

_____

_____

_____

_____

_____

_____

_____

_____

_____

Exercise: Write a detailed long term vision for how you would like the area of family and friends to be 6 months from now.

_____

_____

_____

_____

_____

_____

_____

_____

_____

_____

_____

_____

_____

_____

_____

_____

_____

_____

_____

_____

Good work! Give yourself a pat on the back, look in the mirror and tell yourself "I'M AWESOME!"

Tomorrow you are going to create long term visions of the "relationship/romance" element of your life. Have a great day!

16 Long Term Vision of your Relationship and Romance

What would happen if you had an inspiring and compelling vision for your intimate relationship and romance? What would happen if you were to get so clear about how you want this area of your life to be that you could practically taste it?

Yesterday you applied what you have learned about constructing long term visions to the area of family and friends in your life.

Today, you are going to be applying similar strategies to the more intimate area of relationship and romance. You are going to write a long term vision for how you want your intimate relationship to be 6 months from now, a year from now, 5 years from now and 10 years from now. You are going to begin with the "end in mind" so that you will know what kind of intimate relationship you are ultimately aiming for with each vision you write.

Remember to include concrete examples in your visions. Include: what you see in your future romantic relationship, what you hear your intimate partner say, how you feel in the relationship and what you are doing while in the relationship. The more detailed the visions of your intimate relationship/romance are, the greater the chance you have of creating your visions of romance in your life.

Have fun

> **Exercise:** Write a detailed long term vision for how you would like the area of relationship/romance to be 10 years from now.

Exercise: Write a detailed long term vision for how you would like the area of relationship/romance to be 5 years from now.

_____

_____

_____

_____

_____

_____

_____

_____

_____

_____

_____

_____

_____

_____

_____

_____

_____

_____

_____

_____

_____

_____

_____

_____

Exercise: Write a detailed long term vision for how you would like the area of relationship/romance to be 1 year from now.

_____

_____

_____

_____

_____

_____

_____

_____

_____

_____

_____

_____

_____

_____

_____

_____

_____

_____

_____

_____

_____

_____

_____

Exercise: Write a detailed long term vision for how you would like the area of relationship/romance to be 6 months from now.

_____

_____

_____

_____

_____

_____

_____

_____

_____

_____

_____

_____

_____

_____

_____

_____

_____

_____

_____

_____

Good work! Give yourself a pat on the back, look in the mirror and tell yourself "I'M AWESOME!"

Tomorrow you are going to create long term visions for the "fun and recreation" aspects of your life. Have a great day!

17 Long Term Vision of your Fun and Recreation

W hat would happen if you had an inspiring and compelling vision for your fun and recreation? What would happen if you were to get so clear about the way you want to have fun that you could practically taste it?

Yesterday you applied what you have learned about long term visions to the area of romance in your life.

Today, you are going to be applying similar strategies to the area of fun and recreation. You are going to write a long term vision for how you want the recreational aspects of your life to be 6 months from now, a year from now, 5 years from now and 10 years from now. You are going to begin with the "end in mind" so that you will know what kinds of recreational activities you are ultimately aiming for with each vision you write.

Remember to include concrete examples in your visions. Include: what you see when you are participating in recreational activities, what you hear other people say while you are participating in recreational activities, how you feel when you are participating in recreational activities and what activities you are actually doing. The more detailed the visions you have of your future recreational experiences, the greater the chance you have of bringing your visions of the recreational aspects of your life to fruition.

Have fun!

Exercise: Write a detailed long term vision for how you would like the area of fun and recreation to be 10 years from now.

_____

_____

_____

_____

_____

_____

_____

_____

_____

_____

_____

_____

_____

_____

_____

_____

_____

Exercise: Write a detailed long term vision for how you would like the area of fun and recreation to be 5 years from now.

_____

_____

_____

_____

_____

_____

_____

_____

_____

_____

_____

_____

_____

_____

_____

_____

_____

_____

_____

_____

_____

_____

Exercise: Write a detailed long term vision for how you would like the area of fun and recreation to be 1 year from now.

_____

_____

_____

_____

_____

_____

_____

_____

_____

_____

_____

_____

_____

_____

_____

_____

_____

_____

_____

_____

_____

_____

> **Exercise:** Write a detailed long term vision for how you would like the area of fun and recreation to be 6 months from now.

Good work! Give yourself a pat on the back, look in the mirror and tell yourself "I'M AWESOME!"

Tomorrow you are going to create long term visions for the area of "health" in your life. Have a great day!

18 Long Term Vision of your Health

What would happen if you had an inspiring and compelling vision for your health? What would happen if you were to get so clear about how you want your health to be that you could practically taste it?

Yesterday you applied what you have learned about long term visions to the area of fun and recreation.

Today, you are going to be applying similar strategies to the area of your health. You are going to write a long term vision for how you want your health to be 6 months from now, a year from now, 5 years from now and 10 years from now. You are going to begin with the "end in mind" so that you will know what kinds of healthy activities you are ultimately aiming for with each vision you write.

Remember to include concrete examples in your visions. Include: what you see in your future sphere of health, what you hear other people say about your health, how you feel about your health and what you are doing in order to stay healthy. The more detailed your visions are for your future health sphere, the greater the chance you have of integrating your visions of a healthy lifestyle into your life.

Have fun!

Exercise: Write a detailed long term vision for how you would like the area of health to be 10 years from now.

_____

_____

_____

_____

_____

_____

_____

_____

_____

_____

_____

_____

_____

_____

_____

_____

_____

_____

Exercise: Write a detailed long term vision for how you would like the area of health to be 5 years from now.

_____

_____

_____

_____

_____

_____

_____

_____

_____

_____

_____

_____

_____

_____

_____

_____

_____

_____

_____

_____

_____

_____

_____

Exercise: Write a detailed long term vision for how you would like the area of health to be 1 year from now.

_____

_____

_____

_____

_____

_____

_____

_____

_____

_____

_____

_____

_____

_____

_____

_____

_____

_____

_____

_____

_____

_____

Exercise: Write a detailed long term vision for how you would like the area of health to be 6 months from now.

_____

_____

_____

_____

_____

_____

_____

_____

_____

_____

_____

_____

_____

_____

_____

_____

_____

_____

Good work! Give yourself a pat on the back, look in the mirror and tell yourself "I'M AWESOME!"

Tomorrow you are going to create long term visions for the area of "money" in your life. Have a great day!

Long Term Vision of your Money

What would happen if you had an inspiring and compelling vision of the financial aspects of your life? What would happen if you were to get so clear about your financial future that you could practically taste it?

Yesterday you applied what you have learned about long term visions to the area of health.

Today, you are going to apply similar strategies to the area of money. You are going to write a long term vision for how you want the "money" aspects of your life to be 6 months from now, a year from now, 5 years from now, and 10 years from now. You are going to begin with the "end in mind" so that you will know the kind of a financial future you are ultimately aiming for with each vision you write.

Remember to include concrete examples in your visions. Include: what you see as your future financial sphere, what you hear other people say about your finances, how you feel about your finances and what you are doing as a result of the financial situation you are in. You may also want to include what you are doing in order to maintain this situation. The more detailed visions you have for your financial future, the greater the chance you have of creating your visions of a financially secure future in your life.

Have fun!

> **Exercise:** Write a detailed long term vision for how you would like the area of money to be 10 years from now.

Exercise: Write a detailed long term vision for how you would like the area of money to be 5 years from now.

_____

_____

_____

_____

_____

_____

_____

_____

_____

_____

_____

_____

_____

_____

_____

_____

_____

_____

_____

_____

_____

_____

_____

_____

Exercise: Write a detailed long term vision for how you would like the area of money to be 1 year from now.

_____

_____

_____

_____

_____

_____

_____

_____

_____

_____

_____

_____

_____

_____

_____

_____

_____

_____

_____

_____

_____

_____

_____

Exercise: Write a detailed long term vision for how you would like the area of money to be 6 months from now.

_____

_____

_____

_____

_____

_____

_____

_____

_____

_____

_____

_____

_____

_____

_____

_____

_____

_____

_____

_____

Good work! Give yourself a pat on the back, look in the mirror and tell yourself "I'M AWESOME!"

Tomorrow you are going to create long term visions for the area of "personal growth" in your life. Have a great day!

20 Long Term Vision of your Personal Growth

What would happen if you had an inspiring and compelling vision for your personal growth? What would happen if you were to get so clear about how your personal growth is going to manifest that you could practically taste it?

Yesterday you applied what you have learned about long term visions to the area of money.

Today, you are going to apply similar strategies to the area of personal growth. You are going to write a long term vision for how you want your personal growth to be 6 months from now, a year from now, 5 years from now, and 10 years from now.

You are going to begin with the "end in mind" so that you will know what kind of personal growth it is you are ultimately aiming for with each vision you write.

Remember to include concrete examples in your visions. Include: what you see as your future personal growth plan, what you hear other people say about your plan while you are participating in it, how you feel about your plan and what you are doing in it, and what specifically you are doing while participating in your plan. The more detailed your visions for your future personal growth are, the greater the chance you have of bringing your visions of personal growth to fruition.

Have fun!

> **Exercise:** Write a detailed long term vision for how you would like the area of personal growth to be 10 years from now.

_____

_____

_____

_____

_____

_____

_____

_____

_____

_____

_____

_____

_____

_____

_____

_____

_____

_____

Exercise: Write a detailed long term vision for how you would like the area of personal growth to be 5 years from now.

_____

_____

_____

_____

_____

_____

_____

_____

_____

_____

_____

_____

_____

_____

_____

_____

_____

_____

_____

_____

_____

_____

_____

_____

Exercise: Write a detailed long term vision for how you would like the area of personal growth to be 1 year from now.

_____

_____

_____

_____

_____

_____

_____

_____

_____

_____

_____

_____

_____

_____

_____

_____

_____

_____

_____

_____

_____

_____

_____

Exercise: Write a detailed long term vision for how you would like the area of personal growth to be 6 months from now.

_____

_____

_____

_____

_____

_____

_____

_____

_____

_____

_____

_____

_____

_____

_____

_____

_____

_____

Good work! Give yourself a pat on the back, look in the mirror and tell yourself "I'M AWESOME!"

Tomorrow you are going to create long term visions for the area of "physical environment" in your life. Have a great day!

Long Term Vision of your Physical Environment

W hat would happen if you had an inspiring and compelling vision for your physical environment? What would happen if you were to get so clear about how you want your physical environment to be that you could practically taste it?

Yesterday you applied what you have learned about long term visions to the area of personal growth.

Today, you are going to apply similar strategies to the area of physical environment. You are going to write a long term vision for how you want your physical environment to be 6 months from now, a year from now, 5 years from now, and 10 years from now. You are going to begin with the "end in mind" so that you will know what kind of physical environment you are ultimately aiming for with each vision you write.

Remember to include concrete examples in your visions. Include: what you see as your future physical environment, what you hear other people say about your future physical environment, how you feel when you are in your future physical environment and what you are doing in your future physical environment. The more detailed the visions of your future physical environment are, the greater the chance you have of developing your visions of a healthy physical environment into your life.

Have fun!

Exercise: Write a detailed long term vision for how you would like the area of physical environment to be 10 years from now.

_____

_____

_____

_____

_____

_____

_____

_____

_____

_____

_____

_____

_____

_____

_____

_____

_____

Exercise: Write a detailed long term vision for how you would like the area of physical environment to be 5 years from now.

_____

_____

_____

_____

_____

_____

_____

_____

_____

_____

_____

_____

_____

_____

_____

_____

_____

_____

_____

_____

_____

_____

_____

Exercise: Write a detailed long term vision for how you would like the area of physical environment to be 1 year from now.

_____

_____

_____

_____

_____

_____

_____

_____

_____

_____

_____

_____

_____

_____

_____

_____

_____

_____

_____

_____

_____

_____

_____

Exercise: Write a detailed long term vision for how you would like the area of physical environment to be 6 months from now.

_____

_____

_____

_____

_____

_____

_____

_____

_____

_____

_____

_____

_____

_____

_____

_____

_____

_____

_____

Good work! Give yourself a pat on the back, look in the mirror and tell yourself "I'M AWESOME!"

Tomorrow you are going to begin to develop a strategy to translate your long term visions into your reality. Have a great day!

Your Journey

You now have the starting point and the end point to your journey. Now comes the most important part – the journey itself! The fourth secret to create your ultimate life is to have a plan for your journey.

On days 22 to 30 you will create the strategy that will move you from where you are now to where you want to be. This is where the heat really gets turned up and where the rubber meets the road, because it is time to implement and create the life you have always wanted.

DAY 22 Creating a Successful Strategy

What would happen if you had a way to turn your long-term visions into a reality? What would happen if you had a plan that simply could not fail?

Every good book has an outline and every great building has a solid set of blueprints and over the past three weeks you have been laying the groundwork to develop a successful strategy for your SuperU life.

You:

- Gained an understanding about the importance of your personal core and how its strength can either positively, or negatively, affect each element of your life.

- Developed an understanding of how limiting beliefs can keep you stuck inside of a 'false' sense of comfort, and how challenging these beliefs can help you to live the life you want.

- Discovered that if you separate your life into its various elements, and define your degree of satisfaction in each, it becomes easier to see what is working and what isn't; then you are able to decide on the changes you want to make.

- Continued to magnify your awareness for each element of your life by applying the Personal Core and Comfort Zone concepts to them.
- Defined what is most important to you and then created compelling and inspiring long term visions for each element of your life to ensure that you will lead the life your want in the future.

Now that you have a thorough understanding of your life and what you want to create, you are ready to design the strategies that will get you there. These strategies will require you to set goals, take action, and continually assess your progress. If you are consistent and maintain your commitment to yourself, before you know it, you will be living the life of your dreams!

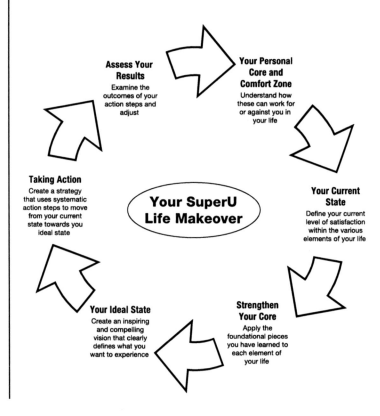

Over the past three weeks you have:

1. Gained an understanding of your Personal Core and Comfort Zone.

2. Defined your Current State.

3. Strengthened your Core.

4. Defined your Ideal State.

Now it is time to take action and assess your results.

You need to have a specific strategy in mind to move you from where you are currently to where you want to go. For example, imagine that you want to go from Chicago to New York on a trip. There are many different strategies that you could use to get you there.

You could drive, fly, hop on a train or a bus, or even walk! Let's say you decide to drive - there are still many different options from which to choose. You could drive alone or with a friend, you could drive non-stop or stop every eight hours, you could drive along major high-ways or you could take the back-roads. (You get the picture.)

The more specific your strategy is, the more likely it is to succeed.

You are going to use two different strategies to move you from your current state to your ideal state in each area of your life.

The first is to: **begin with the end in mind.**

You used a similar tactic when you wrote your long term visions for each area of your life. Keeping the "end in mind" will help you move from your restrictive comfort zone and take action even when you are scared. If you begin with the end in mind, you will be more focused on what is important when you begin to lose faith.

The second strategy is: **understanding that you have finite resources for self-regulation.**

Change can be stressful, frustrating, and potentially over-whelming - especially if you take steps that are too big, or if you take too many steps all at once. Understanding that you have finite resources for self-regulation helps you recognize that you will have a greater likelihood of success if you take baby steps and only change one or two things at a time.

Exercise: Think of a time in your life when you tried to make too many changes at once and as result failed.

_____

_____

_____

_____

_____

_____

_____

_____

_____

_____

_____

_____

_____

_____

_____

_____

Exercise: Now think of a time in your life when you committed to change just one thing. How was this experience different?

_____

_____

_____

_____

_____

_____

_____

_____

_____

_____

_____

_____

Once you have determined the strategies to use, the next step is to set goals to bridge the gap between where you are now and where you want to go. These goals need to be S.M.A.R.T. – Specific, Measurable, Attainable/Achievable, Realistic/Reasonable and Time-bound.

- **Specific** – The single key result that you want to attain with this goal.

- **Measurable** – The way you can measure the result of your goal.

- **Attainable/Achievable** – How achievable your goal is.

- **Realistic/Reasonable** – How realistic your goal is.

- **Time Bound** – The amount of time you give yourself to attain the goal.

Your long term vision will give you emotional ownership over your goals, and together with your strategies, will help you determine and prioritize which goals need to be met.

After your goals are set, the next step is to create a plan of action that will create the results you want. Here you will keep what is known as a *goal chart*, that is simply a means for plotting your course and keeping track of your progress.

Once you have begun the charting process, the final step of your life strategy comes into play – Assessing Your Results.

This final step requires you to assess the outcomes of your goals and action steps and adjust and realign where necessary. As you take action, you will adjust and realign your action steps and goals in accordance with the results you achieve. Similar to how an airplane or a sailboat gets from point A to B by constantly adjusting its course, you will move from your current state towards your ideal state by constantly adjusting your action plan.

You may find, for example, that some goals require you to strengthen certain aspects of your core, while others require you to expand your comfort zone, and other goals require you to become even more specific in defining what you want. Be open to making adjustments and realignments. It is simply part of the process.

Good work! Give yourself a pat on the back, look in the mirror and tell yourself "I'M AWESOME!"

Tomorrow you are going to begin applying these final two steps of your SuperU Life Makeover to the area of "career". Have a great day!

DAY 23 Your Career Strategy

What would happen if you had a plan to turn the long term vision of your career into a reality? What would happen if you knew your plan could not fail?

Yesterday you learned two strategies for turning your long term visions into a reality, how to set S.M.A.R.T goals and how to create a plan of action. Today, you are going to apply what you have learned to the area of your career.

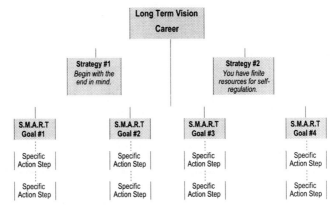

In the preceding diagram, you can see that the process begins with your long term vision and then branches out to the two strategies followed by your goals and specific action steps.

Everything you need to do is outlined in the steps below.

Have fun!

Step One: Reread all of the long term visions you wrote for your career.

Step Two: Start with strategy #1 – Beginning with the End in Mind - you are going to plan your goals backwards so that the end is what you are thinking of first. For example, if the end goal for your career in 10 years is to be V.P. you will start there and then think of what goal must have preceded it (perhaps it was the goal of becoming District Manager of…).

Year 10 to Year 5:

_____

_____

_____

_____

_____

_____

_____

_____

_____

_____

_____

_____

_____

_____

_____

_____

_____

_____

_____

_____

_____

Year 5 to Year 1:

_____

_____

_____

_____

_____

_____

_____

_____

_____

_____

_____

_____

_____

_____

_____

_____

_____

_____

_____

6 months to Year 1:

_____

_____

_____

_____

_____

_____

_____

_____

_____

_____

_____

_____

_____

_____

_____

_____

_____

_____

3 months to 6 months:

_____

_____

_____

_____

_____

_____

_____

_____

_____

_____

_____

_____

_____

_____

_____

_____

_____

_____

2 months to 3 months:

_____

_____

_____

_____

_____

_____

_____

_____

_____

_____

1 month to 2 months:

_____

_____

_____

_____

_____

_____

_____

_____

_____

_____

0 to 1 month:

_____

_____

_____

_____

_____

_____

_____

_____

_____

Step Three: Now that you have a good understanding of all of things you need to do to make your visions a reality choose 3 S.M.A.R.T. goals for you to complete within the next 6 months that will bring you the closest to your 6-month long term vision. Remember to make them S.M.A.R.T.

Specific, **M**easurable, **A**ttainable, **R**ealistic and **T**ime-Bound.

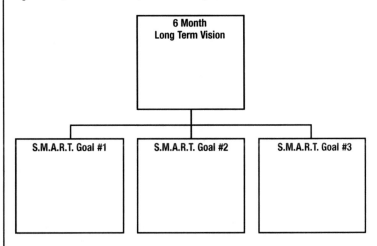

Step Four: Implement Strategy #2 (understanding that you have finite resources for self-regulation) and choose one goal to work on over the next 3 months and design 3 action steps to help complete the goal by the end of the 6-month period.

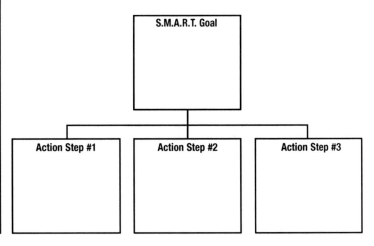

Step five: Chart your progress with each action step. It takes approximately 21 days to create a new habit. This chart will allow you to keep track of your progress over a 3-week period.

Action Step	Week 1	Week 2	Week 3

Step six: Assess Your Results. Reflect on how well you have done over the last 3-week period in attaining the desired outcome of your specific action steps within your goal. If all of the action steps leading toward the goal have been met, then you must design action steps for a new goal. If not, assess what you need to adjust, realign, or strengthen your goals in order to meet the desired outcome. Apply the same steps to another 3-week period.

Step seven: As you progress, remember to only begin 1-2 new goals at a time. Your goals may be in the same life area, or in multiple areas of your life. Ultimately, you are going to have to choose which areas you want to focus on first, and then order these areas according to the importance of your particular goals. The process is going to take time – but the time is going to go by anyway, so you may as well use it to create the life of your dreams.

Good work! Give yourself a pat on the back, look in the mirror and tell yourself "I'M AWESOME!"

Tomorrow you are going to be applying similar strategies to the area of "friends and family". Have a great day!

DAY 24

Your Family and Friends Strategy

W hat would happen if you had a plan to turn the long term vision of your family and friends into a reality? What would happen if you knew your plan could not fail?

Yesterday you learned the two strategies for turning your long term career visions into a reality, how to set S.M.A.R.T goals and how to create a plan of action. Today you are going to apply what you have learned to the area of family and friends.

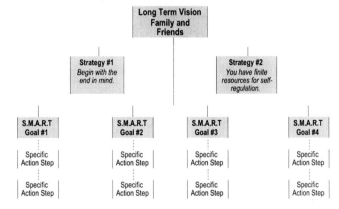

In the preceding diagram, you can see that the process begins with your long term vision and then branches out to the two strategies followed by your goals and specific action steps.

Everything you need to do is outlined in the steps below.

Have fun!

Step One: Reread all of the long term visions you wrote for your career.

Step Two: Start with strategy #1 – Beginning with the End in Mind - you are going to plan your goals backwards so that the end is what you are thinking of first. For example, if the end goal for your relationship with your family and friends 10 years from now is to have *more than enough* close friends and family to rely upon, start there and think of the goal that could have preceded it (perhaps it is a couple of close friends and family members to rely upon).

Year 10 to Year 5:

_____

_____

_____

_____

_____

_____

_____

_____

_____

_____

_____

_____

_____

_____

_____

_____

_____

_____

Year 5 to Year 1:

_____

_____

_____

_____

_____

_____

_____

_____

_____

_____

_____

_____

_____

_____

_____

_____

_____

6 months to Year 1:

_____

_____

_____

_____

_____

_____

_____

_____

_____

_____

_____

_____

_____

_____

_____

_____

_____

_____

3 months to 6 months:

_____

_____

_____

_____

_____

---

2 months to 3 months:

---

1 month to 2 months:

_____

_____

_____

_____

_____

_____

_____

_____

_____

_____

_____

0 to 1 month:

_____

_____

_____

_____

_____

_____

_____

_____

_____

Step Three: Now that you have a good understanding of all of things you need to do to make your visions a reality choose 3 S.M.A.R.T. goals for you to complete within the next 6 months that will bring you the closest to your 6-month long term vision. Remember to make them S.M.A.R.T.

Specific, **M**easurable, **A**ttainable, **R**ealistic and **T**ime-Bound.

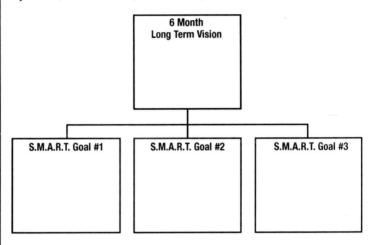

Step Four: Implement Strategy #2 (understanding that you have finite resources for self-regulation) and choose one goal to work on over the next 3 months and design 3 action steps to help complete the goal by the end of the 6-month period.

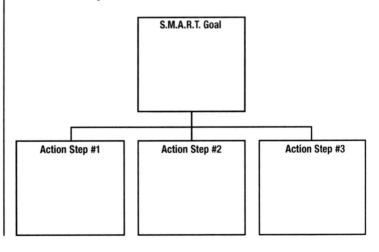

Step five: Chart your progress with each action step. It takes approximately 21 days to create a new habit. This chart will allow you to keep track of your progress over a 3-week period.

Action Step	Week 1	Week 2	Week 3

Step six: Assess Your Results. Reflect on how well you have done over the last 3-week period in attaining the desired outcome of your specific action steps within your goal. If all of the action steps leading toward the goal have been met, then you must design action steps for a new goal. If not, assess what you need to adjust, realign, or strengthen your goals in order to meet the desired outcome. Apply the same steps to another 3-week period.

Step seven: As you progress, remember to only begin 1-2 new goals at a time. Your goals may be in the same life area, or in multiple areas of your life. Ultimately, you are going to have to choose which areas you want to focus on first, and then order these areas according to the importance of your particular goals. The process is going to take time – but the time is going to go by anyway, so you may as well use it to create the life of your dreams.

Good work! Give yourself a pat on the back, look in the mirror and tell yourself "I'M AWESOME!"

Tomorrow you are going to apply similar strategies to the element of "relationship/romance". Have a great day!

DAY
25 | Your Relationship and Romance Strategy

What would happen if you had a plan to turn the long term vision your relationship and romance into reality? What would happen if you knew that your plan could not fail?

Yesterday you learned the two strategies for turning your long term family and friends visions into a reality, how to set S.M.A.R.T goals and how to create a plan of action. Today you are going to apply what you have learned to the area of relationship and romance.

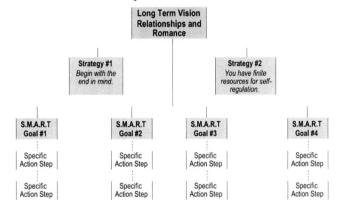

In the preceding diagram, you can see that the process begins with your long term vision and then branches out to the two strategies followed by your goals and specific action steps.

Everything you need to do is outlined in the steps below.

Have fun!

Step One: Reread all of the long term visions you wrote for your career.

Step Two: Start with strategy #1 – Beginning with the End in Mind - you are going to plan your goals backwards so that the end is what you are thinking of first. For example, if the end goal for your intimate relationship and experience of romance in 10 years is to have been happily married for 5 years you will start there and then think of what goal must have preceded it (perhaps having been happily married for 4 years).

Year 10 to Year 5:

_____

_____

_____

_____

_____

_____

_____

_____

_____

_____

_____

_____

_____

_____

_____

_____

_____

_____

Year 5 to Year 1:

_____

_____

_____

_____

_____

_____

_____

_____

_____

_____

_____

_____

_____

_____

_____

_____

_____

6 months to Year 1:

_____

_____

_____

_____

_____

_____

_____

_____

_____

_____

_____

_____

_____

_____

_____

_____

_____

_____

_____

_____

3 months to 6 months:

_____

_____

_____

_____

_____

_____

_____

_____

_____

_____

_____

_____

_____

_____

_____

_____

_____

_____

_____

_____

2 months to 3 months:

_____

_____

_____

_____

_____

_____

_____

_____

_____

1 month to 2 months:

_____

_____

_____

_____

_____

_____

_____

_____

_____

_____

_____

0 to 1 month:

_____

_____

_____

_____

_____

_____

_____

_____

_____

Step Three: Now that you have a good understanding of all of things you need to do to make your visions a reality choose 3 S.M.A.R.T. goals for you to complete within the next 6 months that will bring you the closest to your 6-month long term vision. Remember to make them S.M.A.R.T.

Specific, **M**easurable, **A**ttainable, **R**ealistic and **T**ime-Bound.

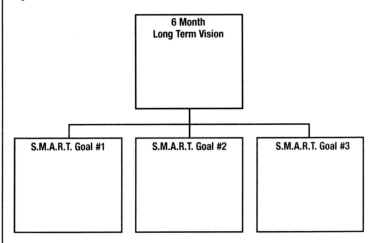

Step Four: Implement Strategy #2 (understanding that you have finite resources for self-regulation) and choose one goal to work on over the next 3 months and design 3 action steps to help complete the goal by the end of the 6-month period.

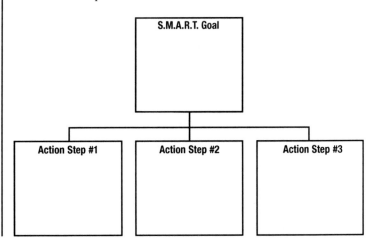

Step five: Chart your progress with each action step. It takes approximately 21 days to create a new habit. This chart will allow you to keep track of your progress over a 3-week period.

Action Step	Week 1	Week 2	Week 3

Step six: Assess Your Results. Reflect on how well you have done over the last 3-week period in attaining the desired outcome of your specific action steps within your goal. If all of the action steps leading toward the goal have been met, then you must design action steps for a new goal. If not, assess what you need to adjust, realign, or strengthen your goals in order to meet the desired outcome. Apply the same steps to another 3-week period.

Step seven: As you progress, remember to only begin 1-2 new goals at a time. Your goals may be in the same life area, or in multiple areas of your life. Ultimately, you are going to have to choose which areas you want to focus on first, and then order these areas according to the importance of your particular goals. The process is going to take time – but the time is going to go by anyway, so you may as well use it to create the life of your dreams.

Good work! Give yourself a pat on the back, look in the mirror and tell yourself "I'M AWESOME!"

Tomorrow you are going to be applying similar strategies to be doing the same with the element of "fun and recreation". Have a great day!

Your Fun and Recreation Strategy

W hat would happen if you had a plan to turn the long term vision of your fun and recreation into reality? What would happen if you knew that your plan could not fail?

Yesterday you learned the two strategies for turning your long term relationship/romance visions into a reality, how to set S.M.A.R.T goals and how to create a plan of action. Today you are going to apply what you have learned to the area of fun and recreation.

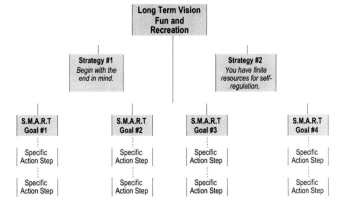

In the preceding diagram, you can see that the process begins with your long term vision and then branches out to the two strategies followed by your goals and specific action steps.

Everything you need to do is outlined in the steps below.

Have fun!

Step One: Reread all of the long term visions you wrote for your career.

Step Two: Start with strategy #1 – Beginning with the End in Mind - you are going to plan your goals backwards so that the end is what you are thinking of first. For example, if the end goal in the realm of fun and recreation in 10 years is to take 3 major vacations and 6 mini vacations a year you will start there and then think of what goal must have preceded it (perhaps taking 2 major vacations and 3 mini vacations a year).

Year 10 to Year 5:

_____

_____

_____

_____

_____

_____

_____

_____

_____

_____

_____

_____

_____

_____

_____

_____

_____

_____

_____

Year 5 to Year 1:

_____

_____

_____

_____

_____

_____

_____

_____

_____

_____

_____

_____

_____

_____

_____

_____

_____

6 months to Year 1:

_____

_____

_____

_____

_____

_____

_____

_____

_____

_____

_____

_____

_____

_____

_____

_____

_____

_____

_____

3 months to 6 months:

_____

_____

_____

_____

_____

_____

_____

_____

_____

_____

_____

_____

_____

_____

_____

_____

_____

_____

_____

2 months to 3 months:

_____

_____

_____

_____

_____

_____

_____

_____

_____

1 month to 2 months:

_____

_____

_____

_____

_____

_____

_____

_____

_____

_____

_____

0 to 1 month:

_____

_____

_____

_____

_____

_____

_____

_____

_____

Step Three: Now that you have a good understanding of all of things you need to do to make your visions a reality choose 3 S.M.A.R.T. goals for you to complete within the next 6 months that will bring you the closest to your 6-month long term vision. Remember to make them S.M.A.R.T.

Specific, **M**easurable, **A**ttainable, **R**ealistic and **T**ime-Bound.

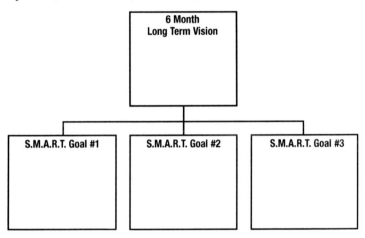

Step Four: Implement Strategy #2 (understanding that you have finite resources for self-regulation) and choose one goal to work on over the next 3 months and design 3 action steps to help complete the goal by the end of the 6-month period.

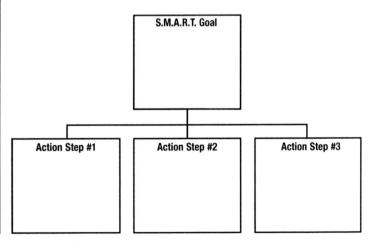

Step five: Chart your progress with each action step. It takes approximately 21 days to create a new habit. This chart will allow you to keep track of your progress over a 3-week period.

Action Step	Week 1	Week 2	Week 3

Step six: Assess Your Results. Reflect on how well you have done over the last 3-week period in attaining the desired outcome of your specific action steps within your goal. If all of the action steps leading toward the goal have been met, then you must design action steps for a new goal. If not, assess what you need to adjust, realign, or strengthen your goals in order to meet the desired outcome. Apply the same steps to another 3-week period.

Step seven: As you progress, remember to only begin 1-2 new goals at a time. Your goals may be in the same life area, or in multiple areas of your life. Ultimately, you are going to have to choose which areas you want to focus on first, and then order these areas according to the importance of your particular goals. The process is going to take time – but the time is going to go by anyway, so you may as well use it to create the life of your dreams.

Good work! Give yourself a pat on the back, look in the mirror and tell yourself "I'M AWESOME!"

Tomorrow you are going to be doing the same with the element of "health". Have a great day!

Your Health Strategy

W hat would happen if you had a plan to turn the long term vision of your health into reality? What would happen if you knew that your plan could not fail?

Yesterday you learned the two strategies for turning your long term fun and recreation visions into a reality, how to set S.M.A.R.T goals and how to create a plan of action. Today you are going to apply what you have learned to the area of your health.

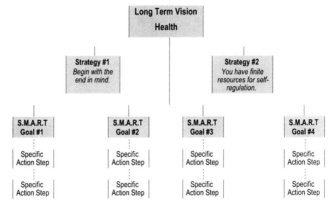

In the preceding diagram, you can see that the process begins with your long term vision and then branches out to the two strategies followed by your goals and specific action steps.

Everything you need to do is outlined in the steps below.

Have fun!

Step One: Reread all of the long term visions you wrote for your career.

Step Two: Start with strategy #1 – Beginning with the End in Mind - you are going to plan your goals backwards so that the end is what you are thinking of first. For example, if the end goal for your health in 10 years is to wake up each morning well rested and full of energy you will start there and then think of what goal must have preceded it (perhaps to set up and follow a regular relaxing night time routine).

Year 10 to Year 5:

_____

_____

_____

_____

_____

_____

_____

_____

_____

_____

_____

_____

_____

_____

_____

_____

_____

_____

Year 5 to Year 1:

_____

_____

_____

_____

_____

_____

_____

_____

_____

_____

_____

_____

_____

_____

_____

_____

_____

6 months to Year 1:

_____

_____

_____

_____

_____

_____

_____

_____

_____

_____

_____

_____

_____

_____

_____

_____

_____

3 months to 6 months:

_____

_____

_____

_____

_____

_____

_____

_____

_____

_____

_____

_____

_____

_____

_____

_____

_____

_____

_____

_____

2 months to 3 months:

_____

_____

_____

_____

_____

_____

_____

_____

_____

_____

1 month to 2 months:

_____

_____

_____

_____

_____

_____

_____

_____

_____

_____

_____

_____

0 to 1 month:

_____

_____

_____

_____

_____

_____

_____

_____

_____

Step Three: Now that you have a good understanding of all of things you need to do to make your visions a reality choose 3 S.M.A.R.T. goals for you to complete within the next 6 months that will bring you the closest to your 6-month long term vision. Remember to make them S.M.A.R.T.

Specific, **M**easurable, **A**ttainable, **R**ealistic and **T**ime-Bound.

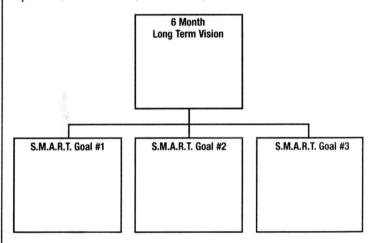

Step Four: Implement Strategy #2 (understanding that you have finite resources for self-regulation) and choose one goal to work on over the next 3 months and design 3 action steps to help complete the goal by the end of the 6-month period.

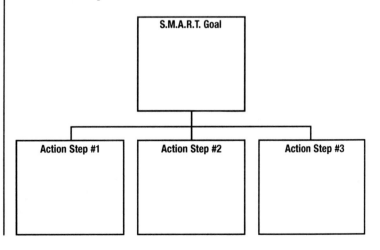

Step five: Chart your progress with each action step. It takes approximately 21 days to create a new habit. This chart will allow you to keep track of your progress over a 3-week period.

Action Step	Week 1	Week 2	Week 3

Step six: Assess Your Results. Reflect on how well you have done over the last 3-week period in attaining the desired outcome of your specific action steps within your goal. If all of the action steps leading toward the goal have been met, then you must design action steps for a new goal. If not, assess what you need to adjust, realign, or strengthen your goals in order to meet the desired outcome. Apply the same steps to another 3-week period.

Step seven: As you progress, remember to only begin 1-2 new goals at a time. Your goals may be in the same life area, or in multiple areas of your life. Ultimately, you are going to have to choose which areas you want to focus on first, and then order these areas according to the importance of your particular goals. The process is going to take time – but the time is going to go by anyway, so you may as well use it to create the life of your dreams.

Good work! Give yourself a pat on the back, look in the mirror and tell yourself "I'M AWESOME!"

Tomorrow you are going to be doing the same with the element of "personal growth". Have a great day!

28 | Your Personal Growth Strategy

W hat would happen if you had a plan to turn the long term vision of your personal growth into reality? What would happen if you knew that your plan could not fail?

Yesterday you learned the two strategies for turning your long term health visions into a reality, how to set S.M.A.R.T goals and how to create a plan of action. Today you are going to apply what you have learned to the area of personal growth.

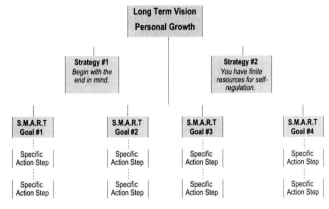

In the preceding diagram, you can see that the process begins with your long term vision and then branches out to the two strategies followed by your goals and specific action steps.

Everything you need to do is outlined in the steps below.

Have fun!

Step One: Reread all of the long term visions you wrote for your career.

Step Two: Start with strategy #1 – Beginning with the End in Mind - you are going to plan your goals backwards so that the end is what you are thinking of first. For example, if the end goal for your personal growth in 10 years is to think positively the majority of the time, start there and then think of what goal must have preceded it (perhaps reading the books Learned Optimism by Martin Seligman).

Year 10 to Year 5:

_____

_____

_____

_____

_____

_____

_____

_____

_____

_____

_____

_____

_____

_____

_____

_____

_____

_____

_____

_____

Year 5 to Year 1:

_____

_____

_____

_____

_____

_____

_____

_____

_____

_____

_____

_____

_____

_____

_____

_____

_____

6 months to Year 1:

_____

_____

_____

_____

_____

_____

_____

_____

_____

_____

_____

_____

_____

_____

_____

_____

_____

_____

_____

3 months to 6 months:

_____

_____

_____

_____

_____

_____

_____

_____

_____

_____

_____

_____

_____

_____

_____

_____

_____

_____

_____

_____

2 months to 3 months:

_____

_____

_____

_____

_____

_____

_____

_____

_____

1 month to 2 months:

_____

_____

_____

_____

_____

_____

_____

_____

_____

_____

_____

0 to 1 month:

_____

_____

_____

_____

_____

_____

_____

_____

Step Three: Now that you have a good understanding of all of things you need to do to make your visions a reality choose 3 S.M.A.R.T. goals for you to complete within the next 6 months that will bring you the closest to your 6-month long term vision. Remember to make them S.M.A.R.T.

Specific, **M**easurable, **A**ttainable, **R**ealistic and **T**ime-Bound.

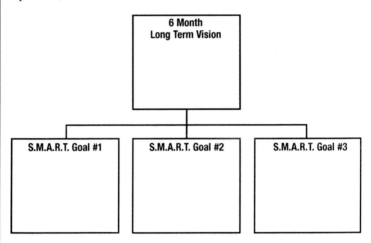

Step Four: Implement Strategy #2 (understanding that you have finite resources for self-regulation) and choose one goal to work on over the next 3 months and design 3 action steps to help complete the goal by the end of the 6-month period.

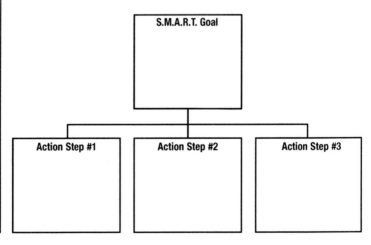

Step five: Chart your progress with each action step. It takes approximately 21 days to create a new habit. This chart will allow you to keep track of your progress over a 3-week period.

Action Step	Week 1	Week 2	Week 3

Step six: Assess Your Results. Reflect on how well you have done over the last 3-week period in attaining the desired outcome of your specific action steps within your goal. If all of the action steps leading toward the goal have been met, then you must design action steps for a new goal. If not, assess what you need to adjust, realign, or strengthen your goals in order to meet the desired outcome. Apply the same steps to another 3-week period.

Step seven: As you progress, remember to only begin 1-2 new goals at a time. Your goals may be in the same life area, or in multiple areas of your life. Ultimately, you are going to have to choose which areas you want to focus on first, and then order these areas according to the importance of your particular goals. The process is going to take time – but the time is going to go by anyway, so you may as well use it to create the life of your dreams.

Good work! Give yourself a pat on the back, look in the mirror and tell yourself "I'M AWESOME!"

Tomorrow you are going to be doing the same with the element of "money". Have a great day!

29 Your Money Strategy

What would happen if you had a plan to turn the long term vision of your money into reality? What would happen if you knew that your plan could not fail?

Yesterday you learned the two strategies for turning your long term personal growth visions into a reality, how to set S.M.A.R.T goals and how to create a plan of action. Today you are going to apply what you have learned to the area of your finances.

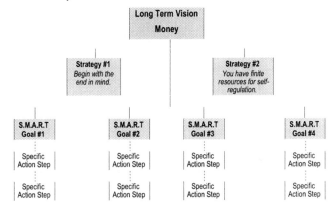

In the preceding diagram, you can see that the process begins with your long term vision and then branches out to the two strategies followed by your goals and specific action steps.

Everything you need to do is outlined in the steps below.

Have fun!

Step One: Reread all of the long term visions you wrote for your career.

Step Two: Start with strategy #1 – Beginning with the End in Mind - you are going to plan your goals backwards so that the end is what you are thinking of first. For example, if the end goal for your finances in 10 years is to have at least $100,000 in a 'reserve bank account', start there, and then think of what goal must have preceded it (perhaps $50,000 in a 'reserve bank account).

Year 10 to Year 5:

_____

_____

_____

_____

_____

_____

_____

_____

_____

_____

_____

_____

_____

_____

_____

_____

_____

_____

_____

Year 5 to Year 1:

_____

_____

_____

_____

_____

_____

_____

_____

_____

_____

_____

_____

_____

_____

_____

_____

6 months to Year 1:

_____

_____

_____

_____

_____

_____

_____

_____

_____

_____

_____

_____

_____

_____

_____

_____

3 months to 6 months:

_____

_____

_____

_____

_____

_____

_____

_____

_____

_____

_____

_____

_____

_____

_____

_____

_____

_____

_____

_____

2 months to 3 months:

_____

_____

_____

_____

_____

_____

_____

_____

_____

_____

1 month to 2 months:

_____

_____

_____

_____

_____

_____

_____

_____

_____

_____

_____

0 to 1 month:

_____

_____

_____

_____

_____

_____

_____

_____

_____

Step Three: Now that you have a good understanding of all of things you need to do to make your visions a reality choose 3 S.M.A.R.T. goals for you to complete within the next 6 months that will bring you the closest to your 6-month long term vision. Remember to make them S.M.A.R.T.

Specific, **M**easurable, **A**ttainable, **R**ealistic and **T**ime-Bound.

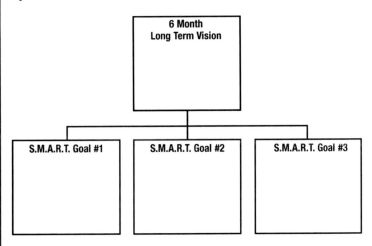

Step Four: Implement Strategy #2 (understanding that you have finite resources for self-regulation) and choose one goal to work on over the next 3 months and design 3 action steps to help complete the goal by the end of the 6-month period.

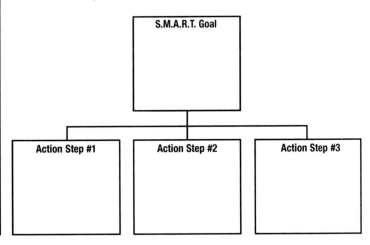

Step five: Chart your progress with each action step. It takes approximately 21 days to create a new habit. This chart will allow you to keep track of your progress over a 3-week period.

Action Step	Week 1	Week 2	Week 3

Step six: Assess Your Results. Reflect on how well you have done over the last 3-week period in attaining the desired outcome of your specific action steps within your goal. If all of the action steps leading toward the goal have been met, then you must design action steps for a new goal. If not, assess what you need to adjust, realign, or strengthen your goals in order to meet the desired outcome. Apply the same steps to another 3-week period.

Step seven: As you progress, remember to only begin 1-2 new goals at a time. Your goals may be in the same life area, or in multiple areas of your life. Ultimately, you are going to have to choose which areas you want to focus on first, and then order these areas according to the importance of your particular goals. The process is going to take time – but the time is going to go by anyway, so you may as well use it to create the life of your dreams.

Good work! Give yourself a pat on the back, look in the mirror and tell yourself "I'M AWESOME!"

Tomorrow you are going to be doing the same with the element of "personal environment". Have a great day!

DAY 30

Your Physical Environment Strategy

W hat would happen if you had a plan to turn your long term vision of physical environment into reality? What would happen if you knew that your plan could not fail?

Yesterday you learned the two strategies for turning your long term money visions into a reality, how to set S.M.A.R.T goals and how to create a plan of action. Today you are going to apply what you have learned to the area of your physical environment.

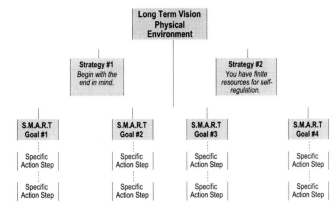

In the preceding diagram, you can see that the process begins with your long term vision and then branches out to the two strategies followed by your goals and specific action steps.

Everything you need to do is outlined in the steps below.

Have fun!

Step One: Reread all of the long term visions you wrote for your career.

Step Two: Start with strategy #1 – Beginning with the End in Mind - you are going to plan your goals backwards so that the end is what you are thinking of first. For example, if the end goal for your physical environment in 10 years is to own a house in the city of your dreams, start there and then think of what goal must have preceded it (perhaps moving to the city of your dreams).

Year 10 to Year 5:

_____

_____

_____

_____

_____

_____

_____

_____

_____

_____

_____

_____

_____

_____

_____

_____

_____

_____

_____

Year 5 to Year 1:

_____

_____

_____

_____

_____

_____

_____

_____

_____

_____

_____

_____

_____

_____

_____

_____

_____

6 months to Year 1:

_____

_____

_____

_____

_____

_____

_____

_____

_____

_____

_____

_____

_____

_____

_____

_____

_____

3 months to 6 months:

_____

_____

_____

_____

_____

_____

_____

_____

_____

_____

_____

_____

_____

_____

_____

_____

_____

_____

2 months to 3 months:

_____

_____

_____

_____

_____

_____

_____

_____

_____

1 month to 2 months:

_____

_____

_____

_____

_____

_____

_____

_____

_____

0 to 1 month:

_____

_____

_____

_____

_____

_____

_____

_____

Step Three: Now that you have a good understanding of all of things you need to do to make your visions a reality choose 3 S.M.A.R.T. goals for you to complete within the next 6 months that will bring you the closest to your 6-month long term vision. Remember to make them S.M.A.R.T.

Specific, **M**easurable, **A**ttainable, **R**ealistic and **T**ime-Bound.

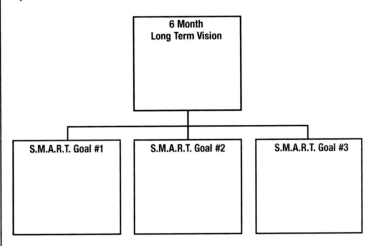

Step Four: Implement Strategy #2 (understanding that you have finite resources for self-regulation) and choose one goal to work on over the next 3 months and design 3 action steps to help complete the goal by the end of the 6-month period.

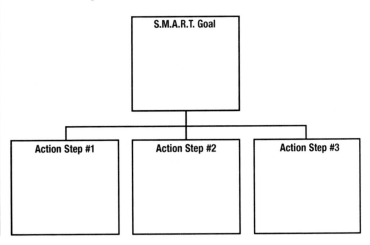

Step five: Chart your progress with each action step. It takes approximately 21 days to create a new habit. This chart will allow you to keep track of your progress over a 3-week period.

Action Step	Week 1	Week 2	Week 3

Step six: Assess Your Results. Reflect on how well you have done over the last 3-week period in attaining the desired outcome of your specific action steps within your goal. If all of the action steps leading toward the goal have been met, then you must design action steps for a new goal. If not, assess what you need to adjust, realign, or strengthen your goals in order to meet the desired outcome. Apply the same steps to another 3-week period.

Step seven: As you progress, remember to only begin 1-2 new goals at a time. Your goals may be in the same life area, or in multiple areas of your life. Ultimately, you are going to have to choose which areas you want to focus on first, and then order these areas according to the importance of your particular goals. The process is going to take time – but the time is going to go by anyway, so you may as well use it to create the life of your dreams.

Congratulations! You have now completed the SuperU 30-day Bootcamp: Your Ultimate Life Makeover.

Give yourself a double pat on the back, look in the mirror and tell yourself "I'M AWESOME!"

Keep on Going!

N ow that you have completed the entire *SuperU 30-Day Bootcamp: Your Ultimate Life Makeover,* your next step is to decide which area of the 8 elements of Your Life is your priority. There are many ways for you to choose. You may give priority to the area that has the lowest score and therefore requires the most work. Or you may give priority to the area you simply feel most drawn to do first. Whatever you do, just do what feels right for you.

Remember though, to focus on only one area for the first three weeks and do not perform more than two or three steps at any given time. Track your results and hold yourself accountable to sticking to the program.

As mentioned earlier, it is going to take some time. For optimal results it is also going to require some support.

In fact, according to the American Society of Training and Development (ASTD) the probability of completing a goal are as follows:

- Hear an idea: **10%**
- Consciously decide to adopt it: **25%**
- Decide when you will do it: **40%**
- Plan how you will do it: **50%**
- Commit to someone else you will do it: **65%**
- Have a specific accountability appointment with the person committed to: **95%**

Notice how the more proactive you are in regards to your goal and the degree of support you receive, the more probability there is of achieving it.

So, get support! Put together a small group and work on it together or work with a close friend. And don't forget, there are many terrific life coaches who you can count on for all of the support you need.

Bottom line of course is TO DO IT!
If not now…when?

I wish you all the best,

Cheri Baumann

Resources

Online Resources:

Coaching — Looking for a coach? Here are some great resources to help you find the perfect one.

- **www.myprivatecoach.com** – The world's leading coaching company with over 70 experienced coaches from which to choose with specialities in business, life, weight loss and relationships.

- **International Coach Federation Referral Service:**
  http://www.coachfederation.org/ICF/For+Coaching+Clients/Find+a+Coach/Coach+Referral+Service/

- **Coach Inc. Referral Service:**
  http://www.findacoach.com/index.html

General Sites — Here is a list of a few of my favorite sites that offer insightful articles and information on personal success.

- **www.actsofkindness.org** - Established in 1995 as a nonprofit organization, The Random Acts of Kindness Foundation is a resource for people committed to spreading kindness. It provides a wide variety of materials including: activity ideas, lesson plans, project plans, teacher's guides, project planning guides, publicity guides, and workplace resources – all free of charge.

- **www.authentichappiness.com** – This site has over 400,000 registered users offering many interesting assessments, questionnaires, and articles.

- **www.healthywealthynwise** – This is an excellent online magazine offering articles and interviews in the areas of spirituality, health and wellness, marketing, business, management, family, personal growth, relationships and career.

- **www.selfgrowth.com** – An all encompassing self-improvement site offering numerous articles in all areas of personal growth and life success

- **www.selfhelpmagazine.com** – This is a fabulous resource on anything to do with self-help.

- **www.soulfulliving.com** – A beautiful site offering inspiring and informational articles on everything 'soulful'.

Great Authors for Personal Success:

Here is a list of just a few of the great authors who have touched my life in some way. Most of them have written so many terrific books, there are literally too many to mention, but I do believe that you will find any book written by one of these authors to be useful and possibly even life transforming.

- **Robert Allen** – much can be learned from this wealth and real estate guru. I particularly loved his book, co-authored with Mark Victor Hanson, The One Minute Millionaire – The Enlightened Way to Health (© 2002).

- **Julia Cameron** – her books on creativity have helped many people truly find their own unique 'artist within'.

- **Jack Canfield** – you do not want to miss his books on personal success.

- **Deepak Chopra** – his non-fiction and fiction books have a lot to teach and I have enjoyed every single one of them.

- **Steven Covey** – his books on personal leadership are world-renown.

- **Wayne Dyer** – has written on many topics to do with personal growth and transformation.

- **Harv Eker** – his recent book, The Secrets of the Millionaire Mind – Mastering the Inner Game of Wealth (© 2005) has helped thousands to create their own 'blueprint of wealth'

- **Bob Greene** – Personal trainer to Oprah, his books offer realistic, practical and an easy to follow regimen for health, exercise and weight loss.

- **Dr. John Grey** – his books on how men and women view the world differently can help you transform your relationship in an instant.

- **Harville Hendrix** – much can be learned from this relationship guru.

- **Gerald Jampolsky** – his writings on love are indeed inspirational!

- **Robert Kiyosaki** – his Rich Dad, Poor Dad series on building wealth has definitely revolutionized the way many are viewing prosperity.

- **Michael Losier** – his book, The Law of Attraction (©updated version May 2006) has taught many how to use the universal law of attraction to get what they want in life.

- **Dr. Phil McGraw** – offers useful information and strategies from everything from life in general, to relationships and families, to effective weight loss.

- **Dan Millman** – his book, The Way of the Peaceful Warrior (© 1980) is a classic!

- **Caroline Myss** – has written many books about health and healing and the tremendous power of Spirit.

- **Suze Orman** – her books on gaining financial freedom have transformed many people's lives.

- **Cheryl Richardson** – offers excellent advice on how to take control of your life once and for all!

- **Don Miguel Ruiz** – has written books about life, love, fear and knowledge based upon the wisdom of the ancient Toltec tradition.

- **Dr. Martin Seligman** – the founder of Positive Psychology, Martin Seligman's books are not to be missed.

- **Barbara Sher** – has written a wide variety of books on how to get what you want and offers many practical tools and techniques.

- **Eckhart Tolle** – offers tremendous wisdom on how to live one's life mindfully and fully in the present.

- **Dr. Andrew Weil** – his books on anti-aging and healthy living should be a part of everyone's book collection.

- **Valerie Orsini-Vauthey** – her 30-Day Bootcamp on weight loss is one of the best I have ever read. It is easy to follow and best of all it offers healthy results in just 30 days!

- **Gary Zukav** – has written many books about the power of what he terms our 'sixth sense'. I have personally read his books many times and learn something new with each and every read.

Testimonials

"I love a how-to book with processes that keep things moving. Cheri's book does just that - it's full of tools you use to expedite your ever-growing success. This book echo's the processes and strategies I used to achieve my personal and business success. Start using this book today!"
Michael J Losier, Bestselling Author, *Law of Attraction - The Science of Attracting More of What You Want and Less of What You Don't*

"Living the life you always wanted and creating the strategy to do so just became easy. Starting with Day 1 and right on through to Day 30, Cheri logically guides you through the entire process step by step. Do yourself a favor - put yourself in her hands, read this gem of a book and get your life on track once and for all."
Raymond Aaron, New York Times Top Ten Bestselling Co-Author, *Chicken Soup For The Parents' Soul*, Founder, www.MonthlyMentor.com

"Clarity is the bases of having whatever you want in your life. This book gives you the steps and a practical plan for getting the clarity which will make your dreams a reality."
Chris Attwood, Co-Author, *The Passion Test - The Effortless Path to Discovering Your Destiny*

"Count me among your fans! Cheri is a well-qualified and highly intuitive life coach. This book will be very effective in helping people move forward toward their goals."
Goody Niosi, Canadian Bestselling Author

"This whole experience has been one of clearing my clutter and helping me redirect my energies. What was most important for me was the clarity the process brought for me. It has provided insight into issues and indecisions that were getting in the way of my creating positive outcomes."
Charles McLaughlin, Canada

"I'm sure Cheri is contagious. Before coming into contact with Cheri I found it literally impossible to feel organized and to manage my very hectic schedule. If you are a typical entrepreneur your biggest challenge is likely to be your ability to gain clarity over your day-to-day schedule as well as your longer-term goals. Cheri will eradicate this confusion from your business (and personal) life and you will instantly feel like a huge burden has been lifted from your shoulders. You would be mad not to seek out Cheri's help!'"
Michael Giles UK